nals

- White with black stripes; dewlap under throat; 'gridiron' pattern on top of rump above tail; belly white: **Cape mountain zebra** *page 49*
- White with black stripes, but yellowish or grey 'shadow' stripes between black stripes, particularly on rump; no dewlap on throat; no 'gridiron' pattern; belly normally striped: **Burchell's zebra** *page 49*

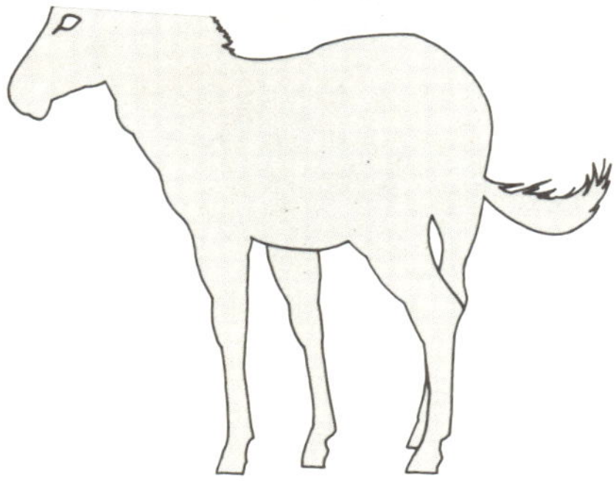

- Silvery grey coat, black tail, dark brownish vertical stripes on neck and foreparts; horns curve downwards, then upwards: **blue wildebeest** *page 50*
- Dark brown, black in older males; yellowish white tail; mane two-tone – yellow at base, black towards tip; horns curve outwards then upwards: **black wildebeest** *page 50*

- Dark brown or black coat; belly pure white; no shaggy neck hair; long, curved, swept-back horns: **sable antelope** *page 51*
- Coat and underparts greyish brown with reddish tinge; shaggy neck and throat hair; long, curving, swept-back horns: **roan antelope** *page 51*
- Pale fawn-grey with dark brown band along each flank separating white belly from fawn-grey back; larger black-white facial markings than roan antelope; straight V-shaped horns; legs black above, white 'stockings' below: **gemsbok** *page 52*

Mammals

• Yellowish tawny coat; yellowish white rump, white extending on to tail base; face yellowish tawny: **Lichtenstein's hartebeest** *page 53*
• Reddish brown coat; yellowish white rump extending to base of tail; black stripe down front of face: **red hartebeest** *page 53*
• Dark, reddish brown coat with purple sheen; no white marks on rump; face dark brown to black: **tsessebe** *page 54*

• Reddish coat, changing abruptly to paler on sides, then abruptly to white on belly; no dark brown stripe on flank, and no white markings on rump and tail; vertical black bands on each side of rump: **impala** *page 54*
• Dark brown stripe on flank separating cinnamon brown back and white underparts: **springbok** *page 70*

• Reddish brown coat with paler brown (but not white) buttock patch; yellowish lower legs; white facial blaze usually broken between eyes: **blesbok** *page 55*
• Rich dark brown body colour with darker patches on sides of head; flanks and upper limbs have purplish gloss; pure white patch on buttock; white lower legs; white facial blaze usually continuous: **bontebok** *page 55*

Mammals

• Golden yellow coat; off-white throat and belly; no black bands down front of forelegs: **puku** *page 56*
• Reddish yellow coat; white chin, throat and belly; black bands down front of forelegs; bigger than puku, and with longer horns: **lechwe** *page 56*

• Greyish with white underparts; yellowish head and neck; bushy tail; short horns: **mountain reedbuck** *page 57*
• Greyish brown coat, white underparts; straight horns: **grey rhebok** *page 57*
• Large white circle on rump; greyish brown coat above and below; horns forward-curving: **waterbuck** *page 58*
• Brownish yellow to greyish brown coat; white underparts; wide-set, forward-curved horns; dark brown band on front of legs (unlike mountain reedbuck): **reedbuck** *page 58*

• Drab dark brown, shaggy coat in male; female same as male, but may have four vertical stripes on side; white chevron on top of muzzle: **sitatunga** *page 59*
• Dark brown coat; crest of long white or yellowish hair along spine; no white band on face; variable colour pattern – in north more white lines and spots on sides of body, in south fewer: **bushbuck** *page 60*
• Fawn coat with white spots; conspicuous white patch above eyes; broad white stripe along each flank; males with branched antlers: **fallow deer** *page 74*

• Slate-grey to dark brown coat (male), rich chestnut (female); up to 14 vertical white stripes in young males, reduced to three or four in adulthood; females have up to 18 white stripes throughout life; white chevron on face; two white spots above hooves: **nyala** *page 59*
• Fawn-grey body (females more cinnamon), with 6-10 unevenly spaced vertical white stripes on torso; long, spiral horns in male; white chevron on face: **kudu** *page 60*

Mammals

• Grey, sparsely haired coat; crest of long black, brown or yellowish bristly hair from head to tail; prominent tusks and facial warts; tail held erect while running; diurnal: **warthog** *page 61*

• Reddish brown body with lighter mane; pointed ears with hair rising from tips; thick patch of whitish hair on sides of face; tail held down while running; nocturnal: **bushpig** *page 61*

• Spots in rosette shapes on body; no black line on face; heavy body: **leopard** *page 62*

• Slender body; narrow waist; deep chest; small, single (solid) spots; black 'tear mark' on each side of face: **cheetah** *page 63*

• Spotted and barred coat; slim limbs; shortish tail; big rounded ears on small head; back of ear has black band separated from black tip by white band: **serval** *page 63*

• Brindled sandy brown to brick-red coat; colour darker down mid-back; off-white underparts; long, black ear tufts: **caracal** *page 64*

Mammals

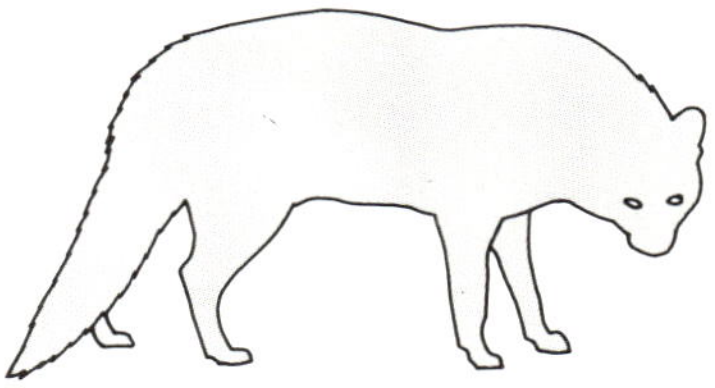

- Black bars, spots and stripes on greyish/whitish background; black 'mask' across and below each eye; lower parts of limbs black; tail black above, but broadly banded below with white: **civet** *page 64*
- Dark to black spots and bars on grey-white background; two black bands from inner ears to shoulders; white-tipped tail banded in black and off-white; black band from behind shoulders along mid-back to base of tail; this can be raised as a crest under stress: **small-spotted genet** *page 87*
- Very similar to small-spotted genet, but has black-tipped tail; black dorsal crest is not erectile: **large-spotted genet** *page 87*

- Fawn-yellow to dull grey-white body, with dark brown or blackish spots; heavy, high forequarters; slender, lower hindquarters; rounded ears: **spotted hyaena** *page 65*
- Shaggy, medium-to-dark brown coat; prominently lighter 'mantle' on neck and shoulders; light cross-bands on legs; black muzzle; pointed ears: **brown hyaena** *page 65*
- Buffy to yellowish white body with several black vertical stripes on flanks; pointed ears; long dorsal crest (raised under stress)on back: **aardwolf** *page 66*

- Reddish brown coat, with black, white-flecked 'saddle' on back; black, bushy tail; pointed ears: **black-backed jackal** *page 67*
- Grey or greyish buff colour; light-and-dark stripe along each flank; broad white tip to tail: **side-striped jackal** *page 67*
- Buff and grey coat; very bushy tail; tawny brown limbs and head: **Cape fox** *page 68*
- Smoky grey or buffy grey upperparts, off-white or buffy underparts; sharp, elongated muzzle; enormous ears; black limbs and black-tipped, bushy tail; black above and brown below: **bat-eared fox** *page 68*

- Yellowish rusty coat; pure white underparts; two whitish blazes on either side of nostrils; small, pale crescent-shaped bands above eyes; almost straight, ridged horns; white rump and white undersurface to tail; upper surface of tail black: **oribi** *page 70*
- Rufous coat; pure white underparts; smooth, pointed, vertical horns; upper surface of tail rufous brown: **steenbok** *page 71*

Mammals

• Greyish buff to reddish yellow coat with white or pale underparts; males have tuft of black hair between base of horns; black blaze on face; front of forelegs dark brown or black; long, narrow ears: **common duiker** *page 71*
• Grey-brown to dark brown coat above, whitish below; hindquarters seem higher than shoulder; ears white in front, grey behind; distinct reddish tinge on fronts of legs: **blue duiker** *page 72*
• Chestnut-red coat; chestnut and black crest on top of head between short, straight, backward-sloping horns; short ears fringed in black on outside, white on inside: **red duiker** *page 72*
• Reddish brown coat flecked with white hairs; white underparts; black band around leg above each hoof; broad pink-lined ears: **suni** *page 73*
• Yellow to brown/greyish coat; white underparts, chin and lips; walks on tips of hooves in rocky areas; short stumpy tail; short muzzle: **klipspringer** *page 74*

• Grey-brown to yellowish grey upperparts; distinctive tuft of long, gingerish hair on forehead, erect when excited; elongated, slightly bulbous nose; short, spikelike horns; tail same colour as body: **Damara dik-dik** *page 73*
• Reddish brown upperparts, abundantly flecked with white hairs; flanks, legs and belly lighter brown; supplementary hooves above fetlocks; short ears and short, vertical horns: **grysbok** *page 75*
• Reddish brown coat flecked with white hairs; horns short, sloping slightly backward; different range to grysbok; no false hooves: **Sharpe's grysbok** *page 75*

• Long spines, cross-banded in black and white; rounded snout; blackish head with no white band: **porcupine** *page 77*
• Short spines; small, pointed snout; overall brownish, but face blackish with white band across forehead: **Southern African hedgehog** *page 77*

• Fawn to dark brown; black hair covers centrally situated back gland; small rounded ears; no tail: **rock dassie** *page 79*
• Grey to grey-brown; off-white hair covers centrally situated back gland; longer body hair: **tree dassie** *page 79*

Mammals

• Greyish coat; very long, black-tipped tail; over 1 m long (including tail): **large grey mongoose** *page 80*
• Thickset, uniformly grey coat; no black tip to tail; about 55-65 cm long (including tail): **small grey mongoose** *page 81*
• Coat varies geographically from grey, through yellow to reddish; slender body; broad black tip to tail; about 60 cm long (including tail): **slender mongoose** *page 81*
• Tawny-yellowish to reddish yellow coat; white-tipped tawny tail; about 40-60 cm long (including tail): **yellow mongoose** *page 82*
• Grey brown with 10-12 dark cross-bands; about 55-65 cm long (including tail): **banded mongoose** *page 82*
• Uniform dark brown coat; about 35-40 cm long (including tail): **dwarf mongoose** *page 83*
• Silvery to brown coat; thin, tapering, dark-tipped tail; black patch around each eye; dark mottling and indistinct barring on upperparts: **suricate** *page 83*

• Dark brown coat (black when wet); light underneath, with white on chest and throat; short-haired, heavy body; no claws on toes: **Cape clawless otter** *page 85*
• Chocolate to reddish brown coat (black when wet); throat and upper chest blotched with white or creamy white; short-haired body and tail; claws on toes: **spotted-necked otter** *page 85*
• Mid-brown to blackish brown coat; shaggy-haired body and tail; smaller than otters; no white on chest: **water mongoose** *page 80*

• Sandy to dark grey coat with darker vertical stripes; reddish brown back to ears; relatively long tail: **African wild cat** *page 86*
• Tawny to cinnamon-buff coat, with distinctive black bars and spots on shoulders and flanks; fawn or cinnamon back to ears; shortish tail: **small spotted cat** *page 86*

• Pale grey coat tinged with brown; long, thick woolly tail; small head, large eyes and ears; length (including tail) 70-80 cm: **thick-tailed bushbaby** *page 88*
• Pale grey coat tinged with brown; black rings around large, round eyes; slender tail; length (including tail) 40 cm: **lesser bushbaby** *page 88*

Mammals

• Cinnamon upperparts, underparts tinged white and buff; single white stripe along each side of body from shoulder to thigh; white rings around eyes; bushy tail; only on ground in arid, open areas: **ground squirrel** *page 89*
• Brown/grey summer coat with whitish underparts; silvery grey coat in winter; tail dark grey with white fringe; only in south-western Cape: **grey squirrel** *page 89*
• Pale grey to buff or rust coat with lighter underparts; only in wooded habitats: **tree squirrel** *page 90*

• Four dark stripes along back: **striped mouse** *page 93*
• Uniform greyish coat; females with up to 12 pairs of nipples: **multimammate mouse** *page 93*

• Dark, reddish brown, with an iridescent bronze sheen; flanks lighter than back; underparts lighter, tinged with grey; white cheeks, and white hairs marking ear openings and the position of the vestigial (rudimentary) eyes: **Hottentot golden mole** *page 95*
• Dark brown, with an iridescent bronze sheen; underparts lighter and duller; buff-coloured bands run from the cheeks to the position of the rudimentary eyes: **Cape golden mole** *page 95*

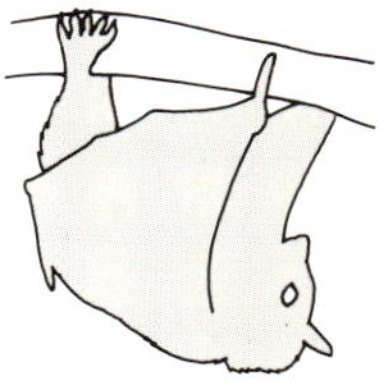

• Dark brown, sometimes tinged with grey; underparts smoky grey; pale yellow-brown 'collar' circles the throat; round-tipped wings dark brown, almost black: **Egyptian fruit bat** *page 96*
• Usually brownish buff, sometimes pale buff; underparts lighter; white patches at base of ears; male has white 'epaulettes' on shoulders: **Peters' epauletted fruit bat** *page 96*
• Dark sooty brown; underparts also sooty brown or a little lighter; head and neck nearly black; ears large, rounded: **Egyptian free-tailed bat** *page 97*
• Light (and sometimes irregular) brown; underparts paler; nose-leaf over face between mouth and forehead: **Geoffroy's horseshoe bat** *page 97*

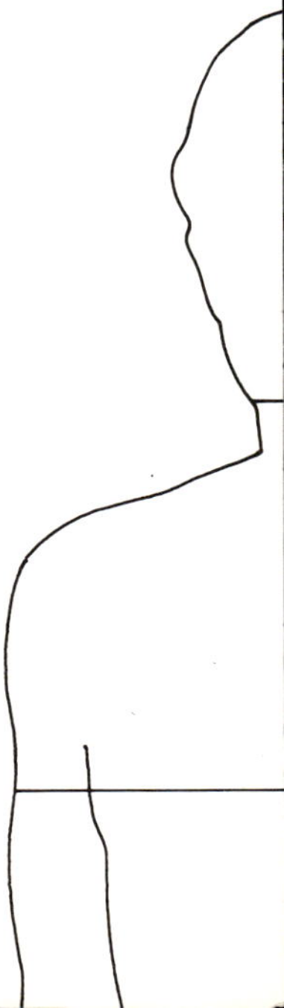

Birds

• Pale grey with black wings, thighs and crest; long pinkish legs; crest shaggy; bare, bright orange or yellow face; long, stiff tail feathers: **secretarybird** *page 108*

• Elegant and graceful; plain blue-grey; darker on wings; top of head almost white: **blue crane** *page 110*

• Conspicuous yellow crest on black-and-white head; slate grey with large, white wing-patch; drooping yellow plumes over wing at rest; bright red throat wattle; broad, chestnut plumes overlie tail at rest: **crowned crane** *page 111*

• Looks like small ostrich; greyish brown above, greyer on neck; belly white; crown black with short crest behind; thick, feathered neck: **Kori bustard** *page 111*

• Brown above with rich chestnut hind-neck; below white with foreneck grey in male, light brown in female; crown black above white eyebrow; black-and-white chequerboard pattern on folded wing; legs pale yellow: **Stanley's bustard** *page 112*

• Wings broad; face feathered; all white except for black wing tips and trailing edges; bill and legs red: **white stork** *page 105*

• Glossy black with white belly; bill and legs dull grey; bill tip, toes and ankle joints red; bare blue face: **Abdim's stork** *page 106*

• Black above, with greenish gloss; white below; white ruff at base of bare, pinkish neck; huge grey to pinkish bill; legs usually covered with white powder: **marabou stork** *page 106*

Birds

• Whitish to buffy with black wing tips, trailing edges and tail; underwing shows row of dark spots along border, with black trailing edge; head naked, greyish blue; bare blue patches on either side of crop; iris pale yellow: **Cape vulture** *page 148*

• Mostly black with white thighs, neck ruff and bar on underwing; breast heavily streaked black-and-white; head naked, bright pinkish red: **lappet-faced vulture** *page 149*

• Pale brown to buff; lower back white; underwing buff with dark trailing edge; iris dark brown; head blackish grey: **white-backed vulture** *page 149*

• Deep bluish grey; crown, hindneck black, foreneck white; underwing pale in front, dark behind; bill blackish above, paler below: **black-headed heron** *page 104*

• Back blue-grey; rest of body, including neck, white; black streak above eye and black patch on bend of wing; bill yellow (orange when breeding): **grey heron** *page 129*

• Slate grey, with deep chestnut-brown head, neck, belly and wrist-patch; throat white; bill black above, horn below: **goliath heron** *page 129*

• Black with variable extent of white from chin to breast; white thigh patches on breeding birds; undersides off-white in immature birds; eyes green: **white-breasted cormorant** *page 127*

• Plumage black with yellow on throat; bare face bright yellow; bill long and slender; eyes turquoise; bill, legs and feet black: **Cape cormorant** *page 127*

• Plumage completely black; bill yellow; eyes bright red; underparts whitish on immature and nonbreeding birds: **reed cormorant** *page 128*

• Mainly black with chestnut foreneck bordered by white stripe: **darter (breeding male)** *page 128*

• Brown with pale underparts; bill greenish horn to yellowish brown; iris yellowish, ringed with brown; slender build: **darter (female and nonbreeding male)** *page 128*

Birds

• Jet black, except for white lower back and white 'V' on upper back; feet and base of bill bright yellow; tail somewhat rounded; wings splayed at tips: **black eagle** *page 151*
• Back and wings blackish; head whitish, shading to bright yellowish-rusty neck and underparts; face mask and bristly beard black: **bearded vulture** *page 148*
• Usually light tawny brown, but varies from dark brown to creamy white; feet and base of bill yellow; tail rounded; shaggy feathering on legs: **tawny eagle** *page 151*
• Largest of the eagles; dark brown, except for white belly with dark brown spots; bill black; eyes yellow; feet white: **martial eagle** *page 152*
• Slaty black above; below pale rufous with heavy black barring; underwing in flight deep russet in front, white behind with heavy black bands; tail banded black-and-white; eyes and feet yellow; *ke-wee ke-wee* calls; found in evergreen forest: **crowned eagle** *page 152*

• Owl-like face; large yellow eyes; head, breast and upperparts black; underparts and underwing white; underwing banded with black; legs and feet white: **black-breasted snake eagle** *page 153*
• Head, neck, breast and tail white; wings and back black; belly and underwing deep maroon; legs and feet pale yellow; haunting *whow-kayow-kwow* cry; associated with large inland waters, coastal lagoons and estuaries: **African fish eagle** *page 154*

• Dark glossy green with bronze wing-patch; bare white neck; bill, bare crown and legs bright red: **bald ibis** *page 107*
• Dull dark grey; metallic purple or green reflections on wings; bill and legs dull blackish; red line along top of bill; loud, raucous call: **hadeda ibis** *page 107*

• Plumage reddish brown above, greyish below; dark brown patch around eye and on centre of breast; dark brown collar on neck; undertail bright yellow; legs and feet pinkish red; iris orange, reddish brown or red; bill pinkish-red: **Egyptian goose** *page 133*
• Plumage chestnut; head grey; (female has white face); in flight wing shows white with green trailing edge and black tip; bill black; legs black: **South African shelduck** *page 133*
• Dark grey to blackish with pale markings; bill bright yellow with black saddle; wing-patch metallic green, bordered white front and back: **yellow-billed duck** *page 134*

Birds

- White, except for black wings and back; legs greenish grey; bill bright yellow with red tip to lower jaw; eyes grey: **kelp gull** *page 141*
- Grey above; white below; head grey when breeding, otherwise white, sometimes with faint grey semicircle behind ear coverts; bill and legs deep red; eyes cream to pale grey: **grey-headed gull** *page 142*
- White plumage with pale grey back and black wing tips with white spots; bill and legs dark red; eyes dark; breeding birds sometimes have pale grey crescent behind eye: **Hartlaub's gull** *page 142*
- White with grey back and upper wing; crown black with white forehead; bill light yellow or greenish yellow, slightly drooping; feet black: **swift tern** *page 143*
- Mostly white; back, wings and rump pale grey; crown black (forehead white in non-breeding dress); bill black (red with black tip in breeding dress); feet dull red (bright red in breeding dress): **common tern** *page 143*

- Neck and underparts rich blue-grey; back rusty brown; head black-and-white; legs yellow; bill yellow at base, black at tip; resonant, *kuk-ka-ROW kuk-ka-ROW* call: **blue korhaan** *page 112*
- Black below and on neck and face, with large white ear-patch and collar on chest; back finely barred black and tawny: **black korhaan (male)** *page 113.*
- Similar to above, but neck and breast buff with fine black markings; loud, crowing call which speeds up towards the end – *kraak kraak kraak kraka kraka rak-rak-rak-rak*: **black korhaan (female)** *page 113*

- All white when not breeding; bill yellow; legs dull brownish; breeding birds pinkish buff plumes on crown, back and breast: **cattle egret** *page 105*
- Slender build; all-white; all black bill; legs black with yellow feet; feeds exclusively in water: **little egret** *page 130*
- Black to slaty black; legs and bill black; eyes and feet bright yellow; quiet inland and estuarine waters mainly in tropics and subtropics: **black egret** *page 130*

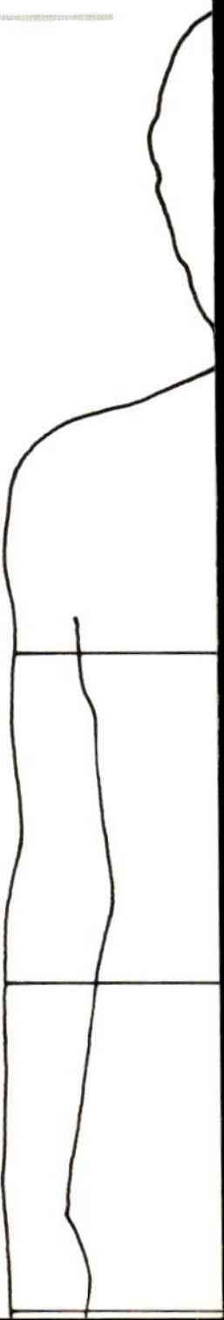

Birds

• Heavy bill; broad wings; black with white collar at back of neck; bill black with white tip; short, fanned tail in flight; high-pitched croak: **white-necked raven** *page 119*
• Glossy black all over; slender bill; bulbous head: **black crow** *page 180*
• Glossy black with white breast, belly and collar on hindneck; heavy bill: **pied crow** *page 180*

• Mostly pale grey; belly white with fine, pale grey bars; in flight wings largely white, tips black; rump white; base of bill, legs and feet bright red: **pale chanting goshawk** *page 155*
• Blue-grey with black wing tips and trailing edges; belly finely barred grey and white; bare face and long, slender legs yellow; tail black with one broad white band: **gymnogene** *page 156*

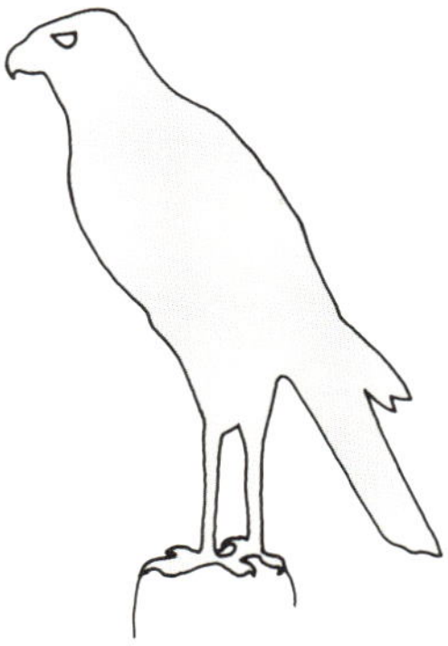

• Above brown, sometimes washed rufous on tail; below white, heavily barred, streaked or mottled with brown; pale band usually visible across breast; underwing whitish with brown leading edge and black trailing edge and tips; likes perching on fence posts and telephone poles: **steppe buzzard** *page 154*
• Slaty black above and on upper breast; lower breast deep chestnut, sometimes separated from upper breast by narrow white band; belly black with white crossbars; tail rufous; underwing black with broad white band; feet and base of bill yellow; jackal-like cry: **jackal buzzard** *page 155*
• Black; back and tail reddish brown; upperwing grey; very short tail; underwing white with black trailing edge (narrow in female, broad in male); face, base of bill, legs and feet bright red; feet project beyond tail in flight: **bateleur** *page 153*

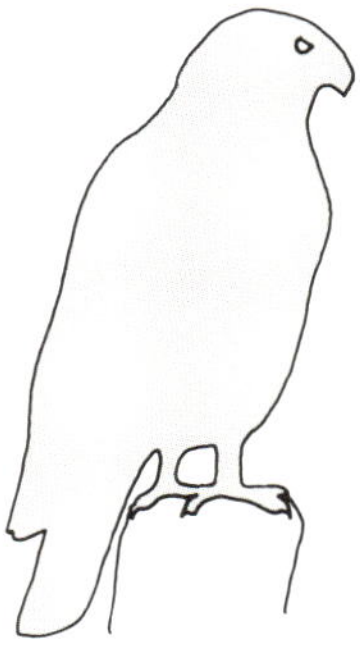

• Dark grey above, spotted with white; below whitish, finely barred with dark grey, and spotted with brown on breast; eyes yellow: **spotted eagle owl** *page 159*
• Grey, finely barred blackish; face paler, boldly outlined with black; eyes dark brown; eyelids pink: **giant eagle owl** *page 160*

Birds

- Bright green with blue wings and tail; flight feathers bright red; crest tipped white; white streak above and below eye; bill red: **Knysna lourie** *page 165*
- Body green with dark purplish blue wings and crest; flight feathers crimson; tail glossy greenish black; bill and feet black; eye-ring scarlet: **purple-crested lourie** *page 165*
- Dull grey, darker on wings and tail; bill and feet black; nasal *go'way* call: **grey lourie** *page 166*

- Crown, back and tail black; wings boldly mottled black and white; broad white eyebrow; below white, mottled black on breast; bill deep red, rather slender; patch of skin on throat and around eyes pink: **red-billed hornbill** *page 174*
- Crown, back and tail mostly black; broad white eyebrow; wings mottled black and white; eyes yellow; skin on throat and around eyes pink; bill deep yellow, strongly arched on top: **yellow-billed hornbill** *page 174*

- Slaty black with white undertail and white streaks on flanks; shield red; bill red with yellow tip; iris red; legs and feet yellowish green: **moorhen** *page 136*
- Plumage deep blue; back washed green; undertail white; forehead shield, bill and legs bright red: **purple gallinule** *page 135*
- Plumage black; bill and frontal shield white; knobs above shield dark red; legs and feet dark green to dull slate: **red-knobbed coot** *page 136*
- Body rich chestnut; hindneck black; foreneck white, shading to yellow on breast; bill and frontal shield pale blue: **African jacana** *page 137*

- Reddish brown, faintly streaked with white above; below greyish, finely barred on belly; breast boldly spotted dark brown; head dark with white throat and eyebrow; legs red; bill black; harsh, penetrating call: **crested francolin** *page 108*
- Brown with black streaks; bare throat, eye-patch and lower jaw bright red; upper jaw and legs black; drawn-out, crowing call: **Swainson's francolin** *page 109*
- Slate grey with fine white spots all over; naked head coloured red and blue with yellowish casque (helmet) on top and red-and-blue wattles at base of bill; staccato *kek-kek-kek-krrr* alarm call: **helmeted guineafowl** *page 110*

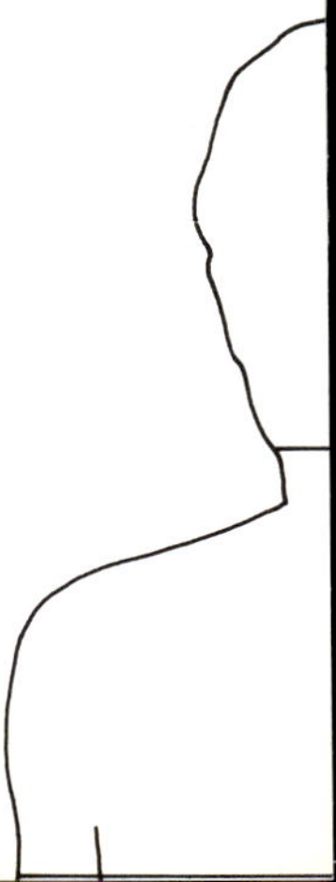

• Brown; face black; bill black above, bluish white below; legs and feet dull red-brown: **speckled mousebird** *page 168*
• Above soft blue-grey; below greyish on chest, shading to sandy yellowish grey on belly; bare face and bill deep red; tip of bill black; legs red; gentle three-syllable call-note, *ti-wi-wi*: **red-faced mousebird** *page 169*

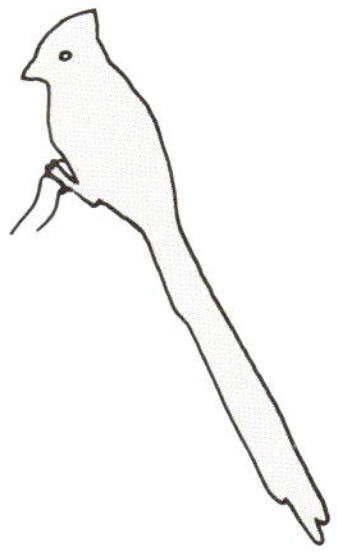

• Above mottled grey and tawny with small black-and-white spots; below white, finely spotted brown; face white, heart-shaped; eyes dark; bill pale; shrill shriek: **barn owl** *page 158*
• Brown above, spotted with white; below white, streaked with brown; eyes yellow: **pearl-spotted owl** *page 159*
• Rich rufous all over, barred on back with black, and streaked blackish below; large eyes; bill blackish; feet whitish; deep hooting notes: **Pel's fishing owl** *page 160*

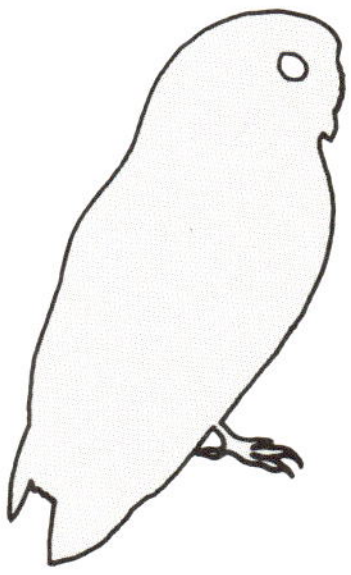

• Back and breast light greyish brown with dark breastband; belly white; crown black with white border; long, bright-red legs; bill red with black tip: **crowned plover** *page 113*
• Mostly light brown; dark brown breastband separates brown chest from white belly; longish bill; top of head rusty in front, blue-grey behind; eyebrow white; legs white: **Burchell's courser** *page 114*
• Sandy grey above, white below; forehead and eyebrow white; forecrown dark; collar on hindneck white; dark line through eye; tail dark with white outer feathers: **white-fronted plover** *page 138*
• Above brownish grey; face grey; dark crown; white stripe from forehead to hindneck; underparts white; one white and two black breastbands; bill red with black tip: **three-banded plover** *page 138*
• Plumage black and white; back and wings grey; underparts black from chin to belly; iris red; bill, legs and feet black: **blacksmith plover** *page 139*

• Slate grey above; chest deep rufous; belly barred black and white; bill blackish, yellow at base; eye-ring and feet yellow; *piet-my-vrou* call: **red-chested cuckoo** *page 166*
• Above metallic bronze-green with broad white eyebrow and white spots on wing and outer tail feathers; below white with broad, metallic green bars on flanks; bill black in adults: **diederik cuckoo** *page 167*
• Crown, back and tail black; rump barred with dull white; wings bright rusty; below creamy white; some faint, dusky barring on flanks; northern (tropical) birds have white eyebrow and white streaks on head and mantle: **Burchell's coucal** *page 167*

Birds

SMALLER BIRDS

• Glossy blue-black all over; rusty red wings show up clearly in flight: **red-winged starling (male)** *page 122*
• Grey head, breast and mantle, streaked on breast and mantle with black: **red-winged starling (female)** *page 122*
• Iridescent black, faintly spotted with white and buff; wing and tail feathers have brown edges; bill bright yellow; nonbreeding birds more heavily spotted than breeding birds; walks briskly: **European starling** *page 192*
• Head, breast and tail black; rest of body rich brown; wing-patch, tip of tail and undertail white; legs, feet, bill and bare eye-patch bright yellow: **Indian myna** *page 193*

• Brilliant iridescent purple; belly and outer tail feathers white; eyes yellow: **plum-coloured starling (male)** *page 193*
• Brown above, streaked black; below white with heavy blackish streaks; eyes yellow: **plum-coloured starling (female)** *page 193*
• Glossy black with bright metallic green reflections; ear coverts glossed purplish; coppery patch on bend of wing; eyes bright orange-yellow: **glossy starling** *page 194*

• Above brown, shading to yellow at edges; below light turquoise blue; throat yellow with narrow black collar; wings, eyebrow and tail green; forehead white; face mask black: **European bee-eater** *page 171*
• Rose red, pinker below; crown and undertail blue; rump green; face mask black: **carmine bee-eater** *page 171*
• Above green; below yellow ochre, tinged

orange; throat bright yellow bordered by black collar; wings bright rufous in flight; square (slightly notched) tail: **little bee-eater** *page 172*

• Dull orange, browner on crown and mantle; wings bluish grey; central tail feathers black: **Natal robin** *page 184*
• Greyish brown above; face black with bold white eyebrow; throat and breast light orange; belly grey to whitish; undertail yellowish buff; tail orange with black central feathers: **Cape robin** *page 184*

• Mottled black-and-white above; below white with one black breastband in female, two in male; broad white eyebrow; bill black: **pied kingfisher** *page 144*
• Above black, spotted with white; below white with chestnut breastband and black-spotted belly in male (reversed in female); large black bill: **giant kingfisher** *page 145*
• Brilliant blue above; crown turquoise; underparts orange-chestnut; white patch on throat and sides of neck; bill and legs scarlet: **malachite kingfisher** *page 145*
• Brilliant light blue on back, wings and tail; large black patch on bend of wing and black line through eye; crown pale grey;

underparts white; bill red above, black below: **woodland kingfisher** *page 170*
• Crown dull brown; back blackish in male, brown in female; rump, tail and flight feathers bright blue; below buffy white, washed on breast and flanks with brownish ochre; flanks streaked with black; bill red with blackish tip: **brown-hooded kingfisher** *page 170*

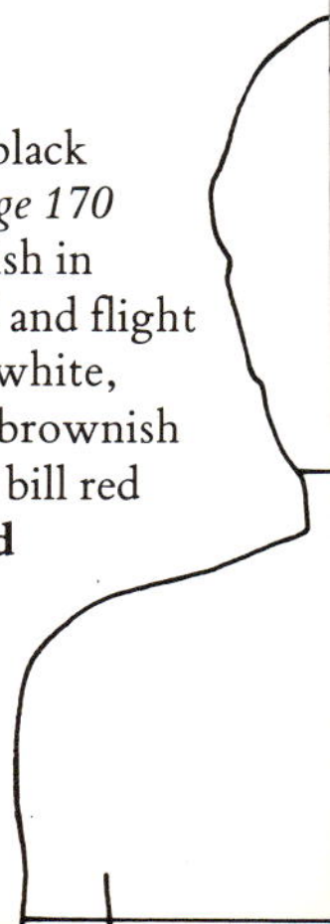

Birds

• Long central tail feathers; long, pointed wings; head and breast plain olive-yellow; double breastband of white and maroon; back and wings brownish with pearly grey spots; belly dark brown. Female rich buff, barred and streaked with black: **Namaqua sandgrouse** *page 115*
• Upperparts maroon brown with white spots; underparts grey; bare eye-patch; legs red; familiar *vukutu-kooo* call: **rock pigeon** *page 115*
• Above deep slate grey with black collar on hindneck; top of head pale grey; below rich pinkish grey; tip of tail pale grey; eyes red; well known for familiar *KOOku-kuROOkuku* call: **red-eyed dove** *page 161*
• Grey, darker on back; black collar on hindneck; tip of tail feathers white; call is a high-pitched, crooning *kuk-KOORR-ru* repeated several times: **Cape turtle dove** *page 161*

• Above blue-grey and cinnamon; head pinkish grey; breast deep rufous, spotted with black, shading to white belly; tips of tail feathers white: **laughing dove** *page 162*
• Long, tapered tail; upperparts grey with dark purple spots on wing; two dark bands enclose white band on lower back; breast of female grey, shading to white belly; face and breast of male black; bill black in female, yellow in male; wings cinnamon (visible in flight): **Namaqua dove** *page 162*
• Greyish green to yellowish green; thighs yellow; mauve patch on bend of wing; bill red at base, white at tip; feet scarlet: **green pigeon** *page 163*

• Bright metallic green; yellow tufts at sides of chest (usually hidden): **malachite sunbird (male)** *page 195*
• Yellowish grey above; below whitish, washed yellowish grey on breast; throat yellowish; outer tail feathers white: **malachite sunbird (female)** *page 195*
• Bright metallic green on head and upper back; rest of back olive; breast metallic purple; belly bright orange; tail black with long central feathers: **orange-breasted sunbird (male)** *page 196*
• Greenish grey above; below dull yellow; wings and tail dusky: **orange-breasted sunbird (female)** *page 196*
• Bright metallic green on head and back; rump blue; breast bright red with metallic

blue collar; belly smoky grey: **lesser double-collared sunbird (male)** *page 196*
• Dull grey above, yellowish grey below: **lesser double-collared sunbird (female)** *page 196*
• Sooty black with scarlet breast and metallic green throat and crown: **scarlet-chested sunbird (male)** *page 197*
• Brown above; mottled on breast and streaked on belly with brown and yellow; wing feathers edged with white: **scarlet-chested sunbird (female)** *page 197*

• Mouse brown with white throat and belly, forming broad brown collar on breast; forked tail; long, sickle-shaped wings: **Alpine swift** *page 116*
• All-black with white throat and broad white band on rump; lives on rock faces and buildings: **little swift** *page 117*
• Uniform light brownish grey; looks silvery at a distance; wings long, slender; tail deeply forked; associated with palm trees: **palm swift** *page 168*
• Above metallic blue-black; forehead deep rufous; below off-white to buff with rufous throat outlined by broad black collar; tail black, forked, with white 'windows' visible

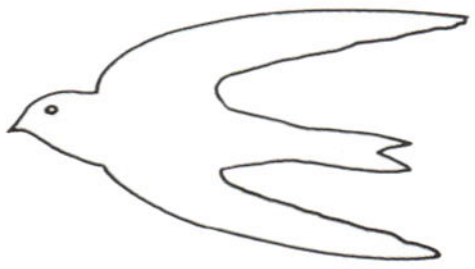

in flight: **European swallow** *page 177*
• Crown brick-red; back metallic blue-black; rump pale orange; tail black, deeply forked, with white windows; below white, lightly streaked with black: **greater striped swallow** *page 178*
• Upperparts metallic blue-black; rump and underparts white; tail plain black, deeply forked: **house martin** *page 178*

Birds

- Body green; head and neck brown; underwing bright yellow (visible in flight only); eyes yellow; emits loud, strident screeches: **brown-headed parrot** *page 163*
- Brown on head and back, with blue rump; breast brown, shading to light green belly; bright yellow patches on crown, bend of wing and thighs; underwing yellow (visible in flight only); eyes red: **Meyer's parrot** *page 164*
- Bright green, paler below; rump blue; forehead scarlet; face and breast bright pink; bill pale yellowish: **rosy-faced lovebird** *page 164*

- Blue-grey head; underparts bright rusty orange; back mottled brown and rusty; tail orange with black centre: **Cape rock thrush (male)** *page 119*
- Similar to above, but head brown, lightly mottled with white: **Cape rock thrush (female)** *page 119*
- Dark olive brown above, tinged greyish; throat white, streaked black; breast olive grey; belly dull orange-yellow, washed olive on flanks; undertail white; bill and legs dull yellow: **olive thrush** *page 183*
- Brownish grey, paler below; ear coverts faintly tinged rusty; rump and tail dull orange; central tail feathers and tips of all tail feathers black, forming black T; deliberate wing-flicking; familiar around farms: **familiar chat** *page 183*
- Black above, including head and throat; breast and flanks bright chestnut; belly, rump, wing-bar and large patch on each side of neck white: **stonechat (male)** *page 120*
- Brown above, streaked blackish; breast light, rusty ochre; belly, wing-bar and rump white: **stonechat (female)** *page 120*

- Above black with white eyebrow, neck-patch and wing-patch; below white with black collar on chest: **African pied wagtail** *page 146*
- Above dull olive-grey; below off-white with grey to blackish collar on breast; outer tail feathers white, conspicuous in flight; very tame in urban areas: **Cape wagtail** *page 147*

- Crown and face blackish; back brown; eyebrow, rump and underparts white; wings and tail dusky, edged with white; breast spotted brown in northern birds: **white-browed sparrowweaver** *page 198*
- Deep buff, mottled black on back; crown deeper brown; black mask on face; sides of belly marked with black arrowheads: **sociable weaver** *page 198*
- Black head with bold semicircle of white on each side; upper back grey; lower back and upper wing bright rusty; wing-bar and underparts white; tail black (female generally duller): **Cape sparrow** *page 199*
- Bright yellow with black face mask ending in point on breast; heavy black mottling on back; eyes red; bill black: **spotted-backed weaver (breeding male)** *page 199*
- Mottled grey and brown on back; rump brown; crown olive; throat yellow; rest of underparts white with greyish tinge on breast and flanks; male always has red eyes: **spotted-backed weavers (female and eclipse male)** *page 199*
- Bright yellow, greener on back; face mask black; back faintly streaked; eyes red: **masked weaver (male)** *page 200*
- Pale greyish brown above with light streaks; throat yellow shading to buff on breast and white on belly: **masked weaver (female and nonbreeding male)** *page 200*

Birds

• Above black; below white, sometimes washed grey on breast and flanks; white bar on folded wing forms V on upper back; eyebrow white in western birds; chestnut streak on lower flank of female; tail black with white outer feathers: **fiscal shrike** *page 188*
• Crown and mantle blue-grey; back and wings russet; tail black with white outer feathers; face mask black; underparts white; female duller in colour with no face mask; tail reddish brown: **red-backed shrike** *page 189*
• Upperparts slaty black with bold white wing-stripe; below pinkish white with rich rufous wash on flanks and breast; tail black: **southern boubou** *page 189*
• Above jet black with conspicuous white wing-stripe; below brilliant crimson: **crimson-breasted shrike** *page 190*
• Black above, with white markings on wings and fluffy white rump; below white; iris yellow, orange or red; female duller than male with white markings extending onto face: **puffback** *page 190*

• Above olive-green with grey crown and nape; tail tipped black and yellow; below yellow with black collar on breast; eyebrow yellow: **bokmakierie** *page 191*
• Crown to mantle grey; rest of upperparts, including tail, green; tail tipped yellow; forehead and eyebrow yellow; small black mask over eye; below bright yellow with orange wash across breast: **orange-breasted bush shrike** *page 191*
• Back and tail black with white wing-stripe and white outer tail feathers; crown grey; underparts and forehead white; black stripe on side of neck; legs, feet and large wattle around eye yellow: **white helmet-shrike** *page 192*

• Head and breast bright red, bordered all round by a broad, black collar; back brownish grey; belly pale, dull yellow; heavy black bill: **black-collared barbet** *page 175*
• Above black, streaked pale yellow; forehead red; large, golden wing-patch; underparts pale greenish yellow; monotonous *klink klink* callnotes: **red-fronted tinker barbet** *page 175*

• Darkish brown above; white below; white crescent around bend of folded wing; clear white eyebrow; bill black: **common sandpiper** *page 139*
• Above olive-brown with clear white spots; below whitish, faint streaks of grey on breast; eyebrow white; bill black and straight; clear white rump; wings dark; tail barred dark and light; legs dull greenish: **wood sandpiper** *page 140*

• Above mottled brownish grey; eyebrow, rump and underparts white; white wing-bar in flight; tail dusky: **curlew sandpiper** *page 140*

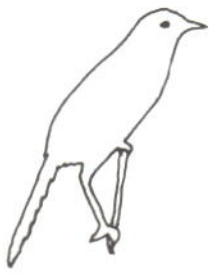

• Back greyish brown, streaked with blackish; underparts creamy white; crown deep rufous; tail dull brown, tipped with black and white; bill dusky with pinkish base: **rattling cisticola** *page 185*
• Dull blue-grey, paler below; crown dull rufous; indistinct buff eye-ring; legs and feet pinkish: **neddicky** *page 186*

Birds

• Black with bright yellow patch on rump and bend of wing: **yellow-rumped widow (breeding male)** *page 122*
• Streaked black on buff above with yellow (male) or olive-yellow (female) patch on wrist; below buff-white, streaked brown on breast and flanks; bright yellow patch on rump: **yellow-rumped widow (female and nonbreeding male)** *page 122*
• Black with bright red patch at bend of wing: **red-shouldered widow (breeding male)** *page 123*
• Streaked black on buff above with red or rusty patch at bend of wing; below white, streaked brown on breast and flanks; wheezy call: **red-shouldered widow (female and nonbreeding male)** *page 123*
• All black with scarlet-and-white patch at bend of wing; tail very long and floppy; **long-tailed widow (breeding male)** *page 123*
• Streaked black on buff above, brown on whitish below; bend of wing orange; flight feathers black; tail short: **long-tailed widow (non-breeding male)** *page 123*

• Similar to above, but smaller; wings brown; no coloured patch on wing; tail short: **long-tailed widow (female)** *page 123*
• Greyish brown above, greyer below, with fine blackish bars; bill, eye-patch and centre of belly bright red; undertail black; *ching-ching* callnotes: **common waxbill** *page 124*
• Crown and back brown; face, throat, breast, rump and tail light blue (paler in female); belly buff; male also has blue flanks; double *tsee-seep* callnote: **blue waxbill** *page 201*
• Deep chestnut; forehead and rump bright blue; throat, centre of belly, tail and undertail black; face violet; (female paler than male and lacking black on underparts): **violet-eared waxbill** *page 202*

• Upperparts buff with dark streaks; below white, lightly mottled greyish on breast; breeding male has bright red bill, black or white face mask and pink or yellowish head, neck and upper breast; female has yellow bill: **red-billed quelea** *page 200*
• Deep red below and on rump; centre of belly and undertail blackish; fine white spots on flanks; back brown; crown grey in southern birds, red in northern: **blue-billed firefinch (male)** *page 201*
• Light red below, shading to tawny on belly; flanks lightly spotted white; upperparts brown; bill blue-grey: **blue-billed firefinch (female)** *page 201*
• Above greyish brown; below barred with buff, white and black; centre of belly buff; head of male bright scarlet; heavy bill pale horn: **red-headed finch** *page 202*
• Head and breast black, with bronze sheen; back and wings grey-brown with green spots on wing; belly white with bold black barring on flanks; bill black above, blue-grey below: **bronze mannikin** *page 203*
• Streaked black and tawny above; head boldly striped black and tawny; below white with buffy breast and blackish streaks on flanks; bill red in male at all times and tail lengthens in breeding season; reddish brown bill in female: **pin-tailed whydah (female and nonbreeding male)** *page 203*

• Black on head, back and long tail; breast brick red; belly, hindneck yellow: **paradise whydah (breeding male)** *page 204*
• Streaked buff and black above; head boldly striped buff and black; below whitish with buff wash on breast and flanks: **paradise whydah (female and nonbreeding male)** *page 204*
• Dull green above, with darker streaks; rump and underparts light yellow, shading to greyish on flanks; black eye-stripe and moustache-stripe on yellow face; yellow eyebrows meet across forehead; white tail-tip: **yellow-eyed canary** *page 204*
• Greenish yellow, greener on back and tail; nape and upper back blue-grey: **Cape canary** *page 205*
• Bright yellow below and on rump; upperparts dull greenish, streaked darker; broad yellow eyebrows meet across forehead: **yellow canary (male)** *page 205*
• Greyish brown above, streaked dusky; rump yellow; below dull white, streaked greyish on breast and flanks: **yellow canary (female)** *page 205*

Tortoises

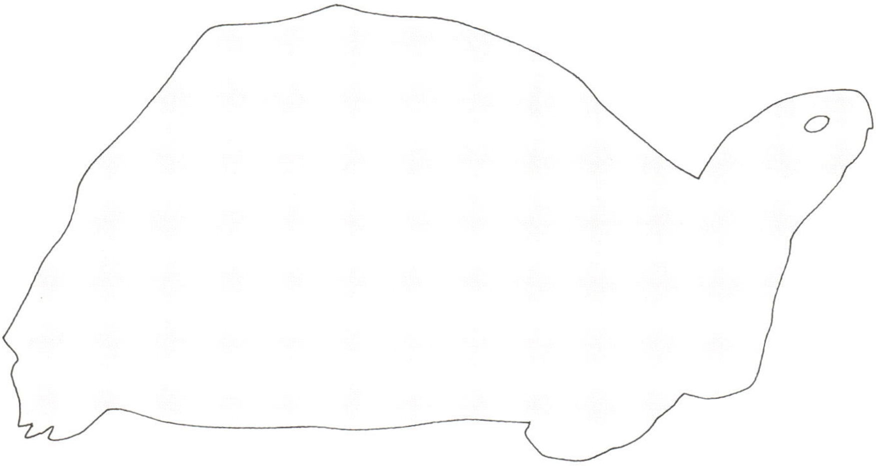

• Rounded, high-domed shell; carapace yellow, flecked with black blotches and streaks when young, darkening often to uniform deep brown with age; two to three horny tubercles on each buttock: **mountain or leopard tortoise** *page 209*

• High-domed, rounded carapace yellow to brown or olive-green, each shield patterned with radiating broad black markings; hinge of cartilage across back part of shell allows rear of shell to close: **Bell's hinged tortoise** *page 210*

• High-domed, rounded carapace predominantly yellow (usually in old individuals), and dark brown or black (predominantly black in young specimens); circumference of shell distinctively patterned with dark triangles; single (not double) spadelike projection at front of undershell: **angulate tortoise** *page 210*

• High-domed, dark brown or black carapace, with pattern of yellow or orange stripes radiating from centre of each shield; major shields raised into 'tents'; distinctive yellow/white horny spur on each 'buttock': **tent tortoise** *page 211*

• High-domed carapace black with yellow stripes radiating from centre of each pyramidal shield; 'buttocks' yellow with no enlarged scale or horny spur; only south-western Cape: **geometric tortoise** *page 211*

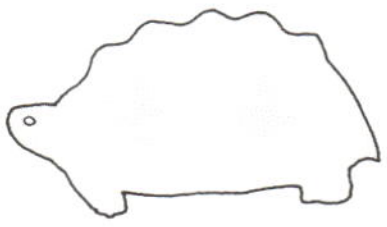

• Carapace dark brown to black, patterned with yellow-brown stripes radiating from centre of each slightly raised shield; well-developed, spurlike projections on buttock; scales round edge of shell are sharply pointed, especially towards the rear: **Kalahari tent tortoise** *page 212*

• Carapace low, flattened; adult males orange-brown above; females and younger males olive-green or yellowish green above with chestnut centres and dark brown or black margins to shields; four claws to each foot: **Cape padloper** *page 212*

• Low, flattened carapace light brown with black spots and streaks (north of Orange), salmon-pink with fine black speckling (south of Orange); five toes on each forefoot: **speckled padloper** *page 213*

• Carapace low, flattened; olive-brown to reddish brown above with no markings; five toes on each forefoot: **Karoo padloper** *page 213*

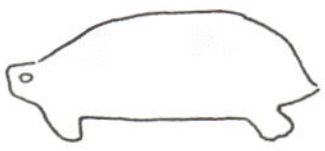

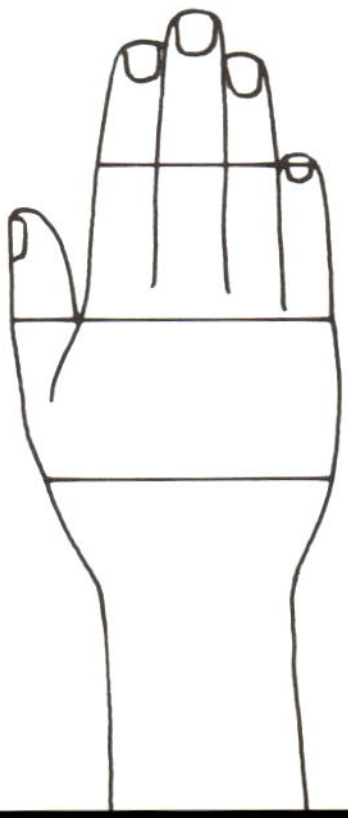

Snakes and lizards

• Triangular head with dark mark on top; body grey-brown with darker brown bars, blotches and lines; average length 3-5 m: **southern African python** *page 216*
• Head approximately same width as body; adults uniform black, red-brown, olive or grey-brown; average length 1-2 m: **mole snake** *page 216*
• Head slightly wider than upper body; blackish V-shape on back of head; grey to brown body with 20-30 dark blotches; average length 35-60 cm: **common night adder** *page 230*

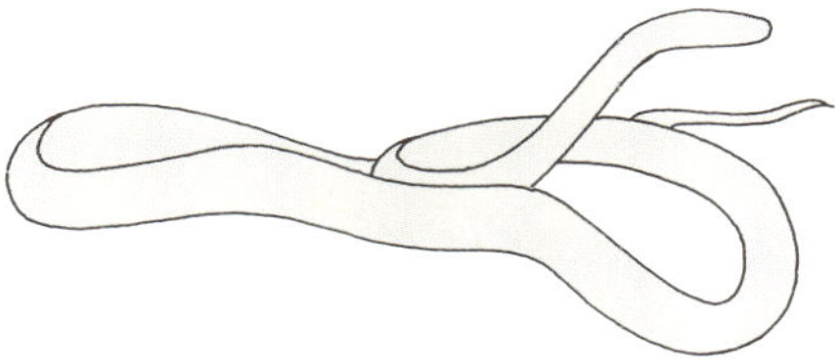

• Grass-green above; yellowish green underparts; white lining to mouth; average length 1,5-2,5 m: **green mamba** *page 220*
• From bright green to olive green (also from light brown to dark brown); large eyes; lives in trees, shrubs; average length 1-1,5 m: **boomslang** *page 220*
• Dull or olive-green, often with a bluish hue; sometimes has black spots over front half of back; underside lighter with white or yellow; lives near reed-lined pans, ponds, rivers and marshes; average length 45-70 cm: **green water snake** page 221
• Grey-brown above flecked with black and pink; green head; lives in trees; average length 1 m: **twig snake** *page 221*
• Olive-green above, usually finely speckled in white; top of head blue-black; upper lip sometimes reddish; head triangular when threatened; average length 50-75 cm: **herald snake** *page 222*
• Olive-brown to dark, almost blackish brown above; salmon-pink tinge on underparts; always near water; average length 60-75 cm: **common brown water snake** *page 222*
• Light brown to reddish brown above; off-white belly; silver-white line runs through each eye; average length 45 cm-1 m: **brown house snake** *page 223*
• Green or olive above with a continuous or broken narrow orange stripe down middle of back; average length 45-60 cm: **aurora snake** *page 223*
• Juveniles alternately banded in cream and dark brown; adults usually uniform deep grey to black, but can have pairs of dirty white rings; belly yellowish or pink; average length 50-75 cm: **Sundevall's garter snake** *page 224*
• Black head; alternate bands or blotches of black and yellow along body; orange-red stripe along backbone; lives underground; average length 30-50 cm: **spotted harlequin snake** *page 224*
• Light brown to dark brown above, with mottled shades; hard, upturned snout; average length 25 cm: **Sundevall's shovel-snout** *page 225*
• Grey to greyish brown with blackish zigzag down back; average length 30 cm: **bark snake** *page 225*
• Yellow-brown above with three rows of dark blotches down back; belly yellowish with dark blotches; average length 60-90 cm: **spotted skaapsteker** *page 226*
• Olive to olive-grey above with brown longitudinal bands; dark-edged forked markings on top of head; average length 80 cm: **fork-marked sand snake** *page 226*
• Silver-grey above with a broad brown stripe down middle of back and another along each flank; cream cross-bars on head; average length 60 cm: **cross-marked grass snake** *page 227*
• Black above and below, sometimes with a paler belly; average length 70-90 cm: **Natal black snake** *page 227*
• Uniform brown above with purplish tinge; underparts grey or cream, sometimes with dark blotches; lives underground or in termitaria; average length 45 cm: **southern burrowing asp** *page 228*
• Usually black or dark brown above, sometimes with each scale white-tipped; underparts white or yellowish white speckled with black; average length 30-50 cm: **Cape wolf snake** *page 228*
• Chequerboard pattern of dark brown rhombic spots above (occasionally uniform brown); dark V on top of head; underparts cream; average length 40 cm-1,1 m: **common egg-eater** *page 229*

• Yellow-grey to dark brown body; sometimes with 7-10 broad yellowish cross-bands; dark throat band; wide hood; average length 1,5-2 m: **Egyptian cobra** *page 217*
• Uniform olive-brown to blackish; mouth lining blackish; narrow hood; average length 2,5-3,5 m: **black mamba** *page 217*
• Dirty yellow through to red-brown or blackish, also speckled brown and yellow; dark throat band in juveniles only; wide hood; average length 1-2 m: **Cape cobra** *page 218*
• Head and forebody yellow-brown spotted with black, but whole body blackens towards tail; narrow hood; average length 1,5-2 m: **forest cobra** *page 218*
• Grey to light brown; back darker brown with black-edged scales; pink or yellowish belly; throat banded black; average length 90 cm-1,2 m: **Mozambique spitting cobra** *page 219*

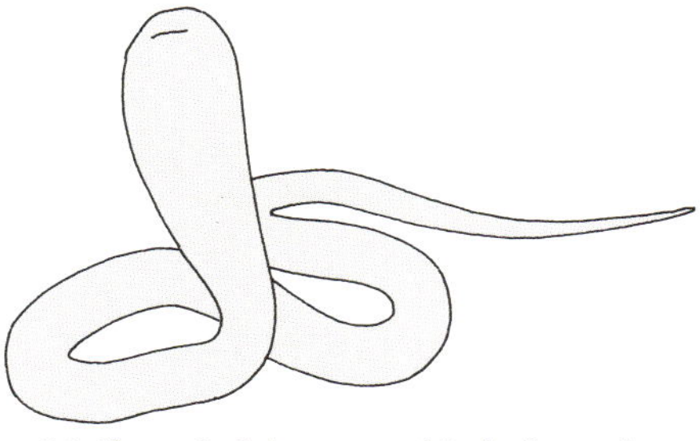

• Uniform dark brown to black above, but eastern Cape and Zimbabwe specimens have yellowish and dark brown bands; dark underparts, usually with one or two pale throat bands; wide hood; average length 90 cm-1,2 m: **rinkhals** *page 219*
• Grey to orange-buff above with series of dark blotches; head and neck black with pale throat band; black V on back of head; narrow 'hood'; average length 45 cm: **shield-nose snake** *page 235*

• Reddish brown to olive-brown above, usually with row of black dots down backbone; sides grey; average length 30-40 cm: **common slug-eater** *page 233*
• Grey-brown to red-brown above; top of head brown-black; black 'collar' around neck; average length 20-30 cm: **Cape centipede-eater** *page 234*

• Pinkish brown to orange-brown above with series of dark brown to black cross-bands; average length 75 cm: **eastern tiger snake** *page 235*

• Back sandy grey to pale brown with three rows of faint dark spots; some have black tail-tips; average length 20-25 cm: **Péringuey's adder** *page 230*
• Grey-brown to dark brown above with two rows of darker, usually triangular, blotches separated by paler band; average length 35-50 cm: **berg adder** *page 231*
• Yellowish or brownish with a series of black, backward-pointing V-shapes down back; fat and sluggish; average length 70-90 cm: **common puff adder** *page 231*

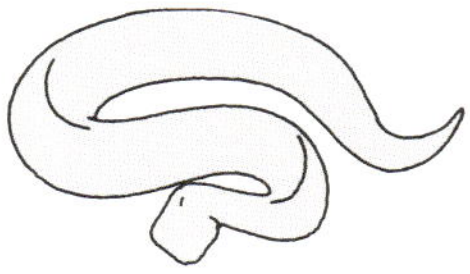

• Richly coloured pattern of oblongs and hourglass markings in black, tan, mauve and grey; head buff; underparts yellow; forests only; average length 1,2 m: **Gaboon adder** *page 232*

• Glossy, dark brown to black overall; head difficult to distinguish; eyes vestigial; looks like bootlace; underground; average length 8-18 cm: **black thread snake** *page 233*
• Glossy brown to dark olive-brown above; underparts yellowish; head indistinct; barely visible eyes; under soil or stones; average length 35-40 cm: **Bibron's blind snake** *page 234*

• Yellow-brown to orange-brown with six black stripes which may be reduced to broken lines or may be lacking altogether; burrowing lizard with no limb vestiges; average length 20-26 cm: **Cape legless skink** *page 245*

Snakes and lizards

• Yellow to dark brown; sides of head and belly yellow; lives in burrows; average length 35 cm: **sungazer** *page 237*
• Very heavily armoured with spines and projections; yellow-brown; lives in rock crevices; average length 21 cm: **armadillo girdled lizard** *page 238*
• Females dark brown with three cream stripes along back; males have bright blue-green body and head; tail red-brown; very flat lizards; average length 20 cm: **Cape flat lizard** *page 242*

• Females mottled in grey and brown; males in olive- to red-brown with purple throat and blue or greenish blue head and forelimbs; body plump; head thick, triangular; average length 24-30 cm: **southern rock agama** *page 242*

• Salmon-pink through green and brown to blackish, depending on environment; usually has pale stripe on flanks; scaly crest down middle of throat and along midline of belly; average length 20-35 cm: **flap-neck chameleon** *page 238*
• Usually leaf-green with broad orange stripe on flanks; scaly crest on throat not

extending on to belly; average length 13-17 cm: **Cape dwarf chameleon** *page 239*

• Grey or brown with four or five wavy dark bands across back; scattering of white tubercles; vertical pupils; average length 20 cm: **Bibron's gecko** *page 239*
• Yellow-brown with blackish cross-bars or red-brown speckling; banded tail; white belly; semidesert flats; average length 6-8 cm: **common barking gecko** *page 240*
• Orange to red-brown above with varied markings; whitish pink underparts; short toes; average length 14-17 cm: **giant ground gecko** *page 240*
• Light-brown or greyish above, speckled with white, black and grey; white some-

times in cross-bands; white underparts; fat tail; average length 9-13 cm: **Cape gecko** *page 241*
• Semi-transparent in appearance; pinkish upperparts, with darker lines forming irregular rectangles along backbone; blue-grey patch over eyes; pink belly; only in Namibia's coastal desert; average length 10-12 cm: **web-footed gecko** *page 241*

• Pale brown to red-brown above with light stripes; breeding males yellow on throat and around vent; average length 15-23 cm: **Knox's desert lizard** *page 243*
• Grey-brown with three light stripes along back; fat-bodied; common, even in suburban gardens; average length 22-27 cm: **Cape skink** *page 243*

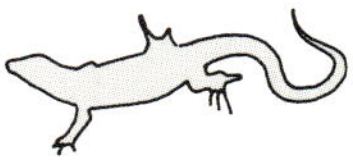

• Light glossy brown above, finely speckled in dark brown; thick tail; short legs; average length 15 cm: **Sundevall's writhing skink** *page 244*

• Silver-grey above, stippled with brown; no forelegs; two tiny hindlegs; average length 12-14 cm: **silvery dwarf burrowing skink** *page 244*
• Olive-brown with two darker stripes

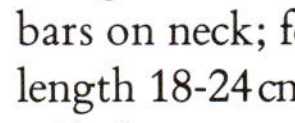

along sides of back; dark, vertical bars on neck; four tiny legs; average length 18-24 cm: **common long-tailed seps** page 245

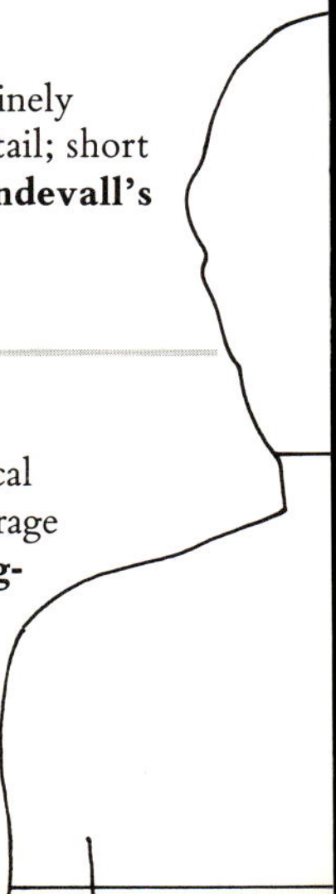

Frogs and toads

- Heavy, squat body with warty, dry skin; blunt, rounded snout; irregular, asymmetrical dark brown/dark red blotches on lighter brown back; whitish belly, usually with small black spots; warts often bulbous: **Karoo toad** *page 248*
- Body squat with warty, dry skin; blunt, rounded snout; usually three to four paired, dark brown blotches down back; belly whitish and never with spots; warts smallish, never large and bulbous: **guttural toad** *page 249*

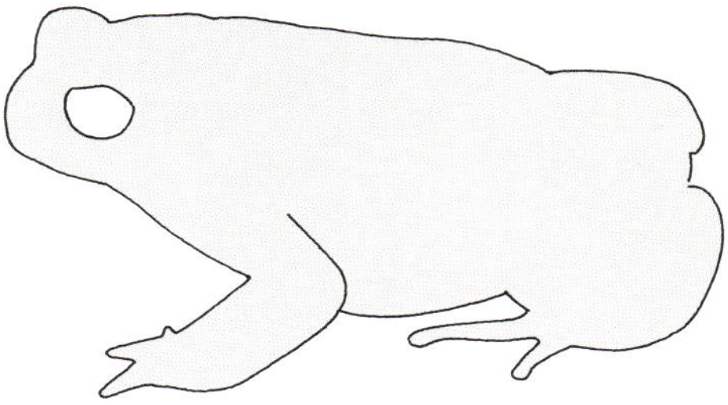

- Bulbous eyes; long, sharp snout; well-developed hindlegs for jumping; green to dark brown, usually with darker blotches; webbing on longest toe does not reach joint of last toe-bone: **common river frog** *page 250*
- Bulbous eyes; long, sharp snout; well-developed hindlegs; green to dark brown with darker blotches; webbing on longest toe almost reaches toe-tip: **Cape river frog** *page 250*
- Bulbous eyes; long, sharp snout; well-developed hindlegs; colour variable but often olive-green above with symmetrically arranged brown spots; smaller and more slender than Cape or common river frogs; toes virtually unwebbed: **clicking grass frog** *page 251*

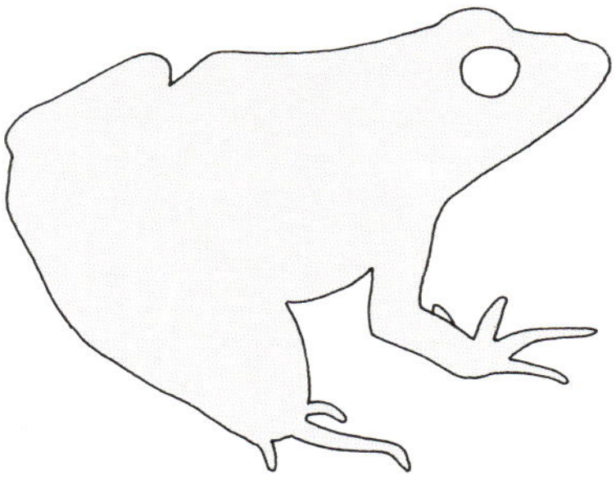

- Small, slender; well-developed jumping hindlimbs; upperparts usually translucent green, but can be yellow or light brown; underparts white or pale green; round sucker at tip of each finger and toe: **water lily frog** *page 253*
- Small, slender; well-developed jumping hindlimbs; upperparts variable; eastern Cape brown with dark-edged silver spots; Natal northwards variable with perhaps black, white, yellow or red stripes or spots; whitish below, but red on undersides of legs and digits; round 'sucker' at tip of each finger and toe: **painted reed frog** *page 253*

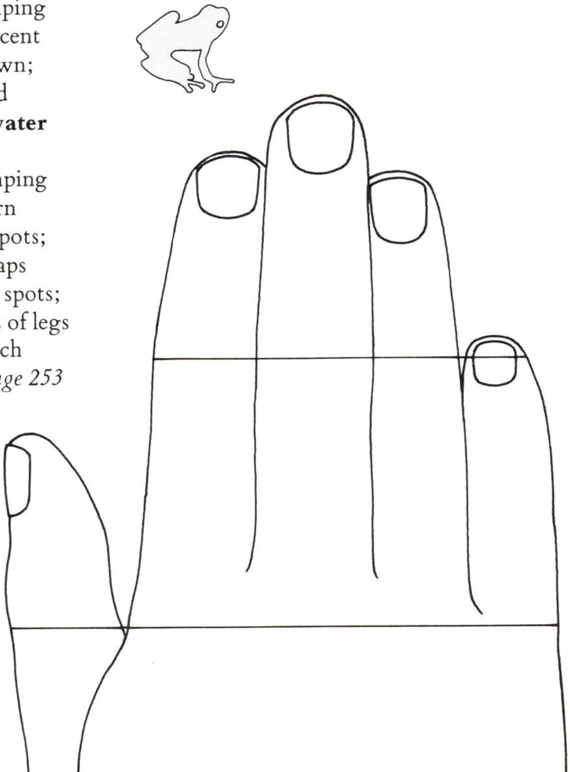

Freshwater fishes

• Silver-olive to bronze-yellow; belly yellowish silver to yellow; anal fin orange; young fish uniformly silver; large mouth with thick lips; two pairs of short barbels; found only in Orange-Vaal river system: **largemouth yellowfish** *page 256*
• Golden olive to yellowish above; below cream to silver; young fish silvery with dark spots or broken vertical bars on flanks; six branched rays in anal fin; thin lips; long, narrow snout; two pairs of barbels; in Berg and Breë river systems: **whitefish** *page 257*

• Green along back; flanks silver; belly grey-white; often three darkish blotches on each flank; breeding males turn dark bluish black above, whiter on throat and chest, with scarlet-tipped dorsal, anal and tail fins: **Mozambique tilapia** *page 258*
• Upperparts olive with light-brown edges to scales; dorsal fin has a red margin; throat and belly of adults red; lower half of tail red or yellow, and green on top; juveniles silver: **redbreast tilapia** *page 258*
• Silver to olive-green; up to nine vertical stripes of darker green or grey; when breeding, stripes become more intense, horizontal stripes form across snout, and circular stripe runs over forehead. In male dorsal fin and tail become edged with red, and blue-green spots appear on dorsal and anal fins: **banded tilapia** *page 259*
• Deep-bodied; dorsal surface olive; flanks orange; belly pale olive or orange; younger fish in particular have five dark, vertical bars on flanks; distinctive black flap on upper corner of gill-covers; lower part of gill-cover blue; dorsal and anal fins large; tail fin slightly forked: **bluegill sunfish** *page 259*

• Silver, shading to olive-brown along back; small black spots over entire body; often pink or red stripe along each flank; slightly forked caudal fin: **rainbow trout** *page 262*
• Silvery brown, darker on back; back and flanks covered with dark brown spots; a few larger reddish spots, surrounded by bluish rings along each flank; no scales on head; truncated caudal fin: **brown trout** *page 262*

• Dark olive above, lighter on flanks with a series of dark blotches; juveniles have dark band on flanks; belly white; eyes red; large mouth with bottom jaw extending beyond upper jaw: **largemouth bass** *page 261*
• Dark olive above, lighter on flanks with faint vertical bars; belly almost white; juveniles have dark bars on tail; pointed snout with thin lips: **smallmouth bass** *page 261*

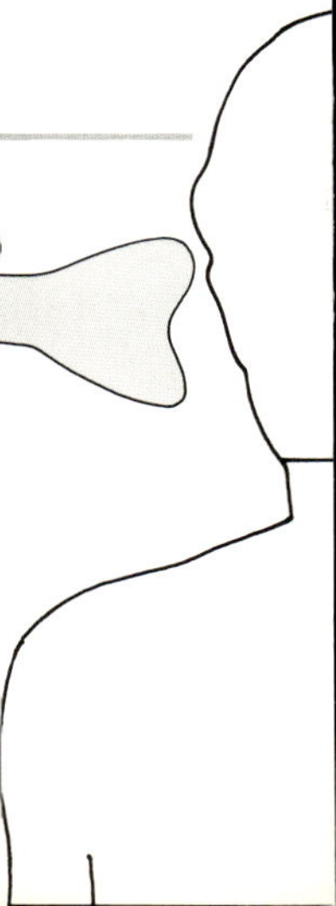

Marine fishes

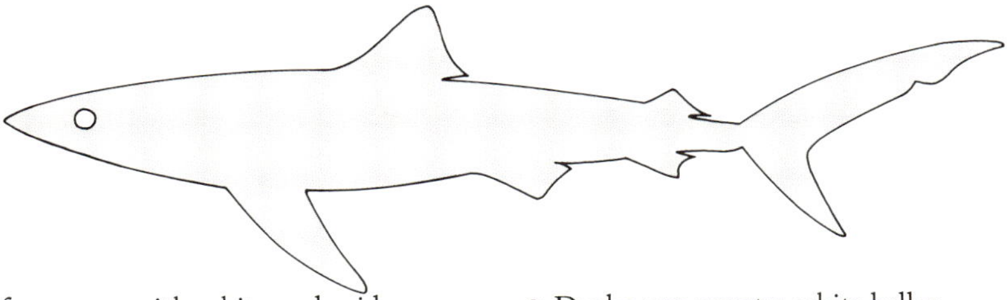

• Uniform grey with white undersides; stocky body; blunt snout; often found in fresh water: **Zambezi shark** *page 268*

• Dusky upperparts; white belly; streamlined body; distinct interdorsal ridge; pointed snout: **dusky shark** *page 268*

• Disc-shaped body; slightly rounded snout; dorsal surface rich golden brown with blue markings; poisonous spine midway along tail: **blue stingray** *page 272*
• Diamond-shaped, chocolate brown body; pale underside; head raised above level of body: **eagleray** *page 272*
• Diamond-shaped body with sharply pointed snout; dorsal surface grey to brown, occasionally with white spots; white undersides; spines on long tail: **spearnose skate** *page 273*

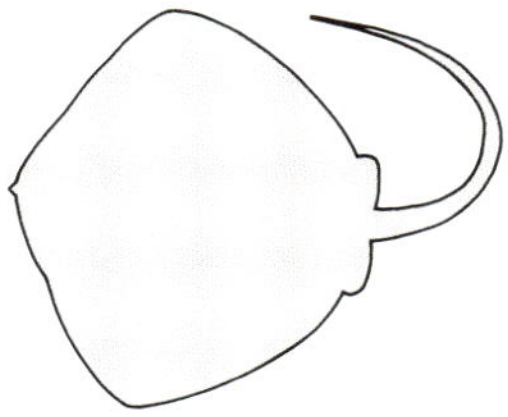

• Disc-shaped body chocolate brown, mottled with irregular blotches; short, stocky tail; pale underside; small eyes on top of head: **marbled electric ray** *page 273*

• Blue-grey body with silver sides; irregular, dark vertical bars on flanks; distinct, wavy lateral line dips between second dorsal fin and tail fin; south and west coast: **king mackerel** *page 274*
• Elongated, compressed, mainly silver body; dorsal surface grey-blue; underside white; conspicuous, wavy lateral line; prominent dorsal spines in single, long dorsal fin; fins dusky to black; east coast: **snoek** *page 275*

• Robust body with depressed head; upper body blue-green, sometimes with narrow bronze band along flanks; sharply forked, yellowish tail fin: **Cape yellowtail** *page 277*
• Large, elongated body; conspicuous lateral line from gill to tail; small scales give a smooth-skinned appearance; ventral surface slopes down to pronounced ventral fin; deeply forked, dusky tail: **garrick** *page 278*
• Elongated, compressed body; prominent lower jaw; sharp, compressed teeth; bluish green dorsally, silvery below: **elf** *page 278*

Marine fishes

• Silvery body with pink sheen on head; black blotch at base of pectoral fin; fins dusky; short, rounded tail: **kob** *page 279*
• Elongated, robust fish; body silvery, but bluish to copper-coloured above; mouth and inner surface of gill covers yellow; tail fin concave: **geelbek** *page 279*

• Deep-bodied with steep forehead; silvery pink overall, darker above; five to seven darker red vertical bars on sides; numerous dark blotches on body: **red stumpnose** *page 280*
• Deep-bodied; pinkish red; characteristic black spot at base of dorsal fin; short blue line below each eye: **dageraad** *page 280*
• Orange body; white saddle over middle of back; white bar on gill covers; shallow forehead; blue line joining eyes: **roman** *page 281*

• Very steep forehead; rosy red body, with iridescent blue spots in live specimens; prominent hump above eyes; blue bar below each eye: **slinger** *page 284*

• Small body; silvery pink overall, belly white; red forehead and pinkish fins; big eyes: **carpenter** *page 281*
• Large, robust body; light red to bronze (some with yellow undersides); fins darker red; slightly extended snout; bony ridge between eyes: **red steenbras** *page 282*
• Moderately elongated body; forehead smoothly convex; upperparts pinkish red with blue sheen; conspicuous black mark on lateral line below fifth and sixth dorsal spines: **seventyfour** *page 282*
• Silvery sheen overall, pinkish above, white below; about five broad, vertical, reddish bars on flanks; bluish sheen on pelvic and anal fins: **santer** *page 284*
• Deep-bodied; rosy pink overall, but bluish sheen in freshly caught specimens; six to eight reddish vertical bars on flanks; snout slightly concave; fins pink: **Englishman** *page 285*

• Silvery grey with white underside; may be completely black in muddy regions; sloping forehead and pointed snout; well-developed spines in dorsal and anal fins: **river bream** *page 290*
• Silvery body with five or more dark, vertical bars; deep forehead and blunt snout; dusky fins: **white stumpnose** *page 296*
• Silvery grey with golden centre to each scale, showing up as longitudinal lines along flanks; fins yellow, fading with age; rounded dorsal profile: **Natal stumpnose** *page 297*

• Robust, oval-shaped body; large head; blunt snout; silvery grey colour (darkens after death), with faint, longitudinal stripes: **white musselcracker** *page 283*
• Large, fleshy nose in adults; deep-bellied, robust body; sooty grey to black; juveniles greenish brown: **black musselcracker** *page 283*

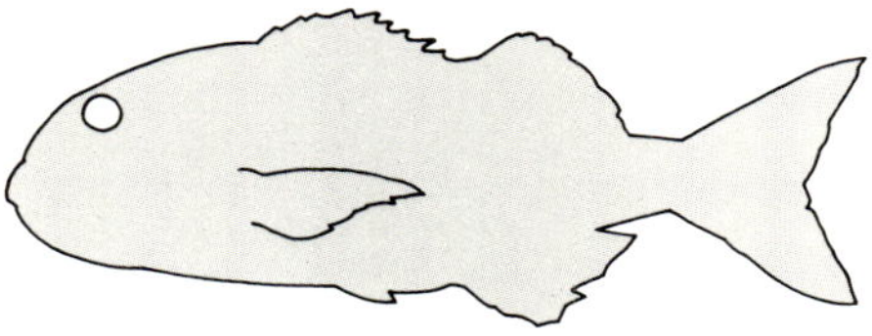

Marine fishes

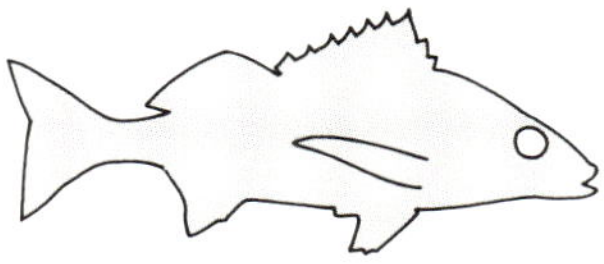

• Long, sloping forehead and pointed snout; bright silver overall, paler below; irregular rows of small, dark brown spots on upper half of body; larger black blotch on each gill: **spotted grunter** *page 291*
• Long, sloping forehead; piglike snout with small mouth; silvery grey above, white below; mother-of-pearl sheen overall; after death about seven cross-bars visible on flanks: **white steenbras** *page 291*

• Silver-bronze to black; robust and deep-bodied; seven to nine vertical stripes on each flank visible underwater; prominent spines on fins: thick lips; pronounced, rounded snout; stout, slightly concave tail fin: **galjoen** *page 294*
• Silvery grey, some specimens with vertical, dark bars on flanks; moderately compressed body; smooth dorsal profile; dusky grey fins; slightly forked tail fin; pointed snout: **stonebream** *page 297*

• Silver, oval-shaped body; pointed snout; distinctive black saddle on the caudal peduncle (the narrow section attaching the tail fin to the body); juveniles marked with 8-10 vertical bars: **blacktail** *page 295*
• Oval-shaped, golden-silvery body; five broad, black, vertical bars on each flank; black bar through each eye; fleshy snout; forked tail fin: **zebra** *page 295*

• Body silver, spindle-shaped; dorsal surface bluish and belly white; row of 10-15 dark spots along flanks; fins spineless; tail deeply forked: **South African pilchard** *page 298*
• Elongate body distinctly torpedo-shaped; pointed snout; dorsal colouring brilliant blue-green with black zigzag lines; lower sides silvery white; fins yellowish; wide mouth: **mackerel** *page 299*

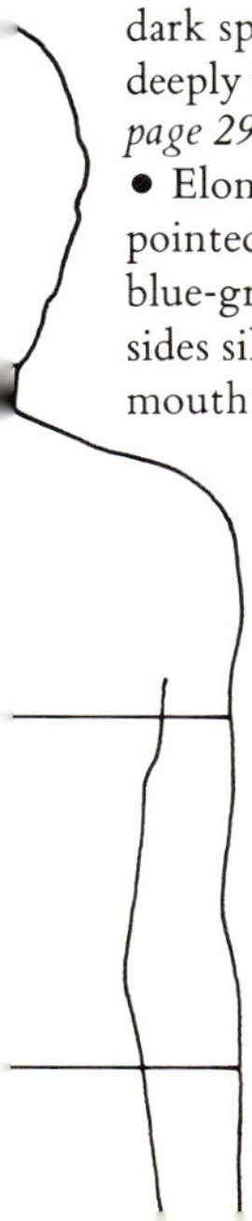

Spiders, scorpions and others

• Olive to yellow to blackish; large pincers; long, thin tail: **burrowing scorpion** *page 321*
• Yellowish, often with brown markings; small pincers; large tail: **bark scorpion** *page 321*
• Yellow to dark brown; thick tail; ridges on first two tail segments; largest of all scorpions: **thick-tail scorpion** *page 322*
• Yellowish with black markings on abdomen; large, short sting; thin pincers: **sand-dwelling scorpion** *page 322*

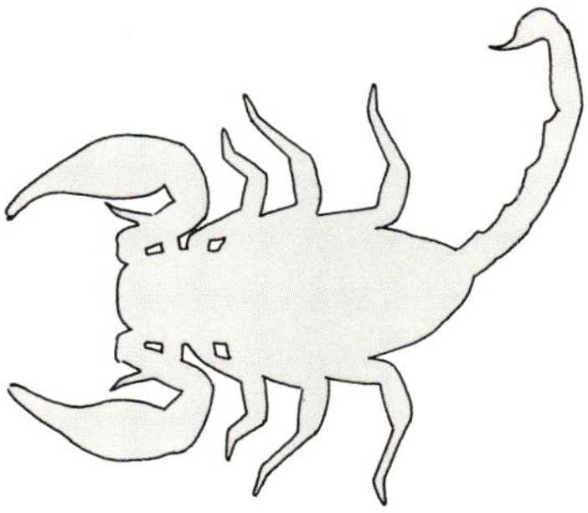

• Light to dark brown; long, fine hairs covering body; huge jaws almost a third of total body length: **sun spider** *page 323*
• Black-and-white or grey-and-white, occasionally brown or brown-and-white; male more brightly coloured than female; squat body; moves by jumping: **jumping spider** *page 325*

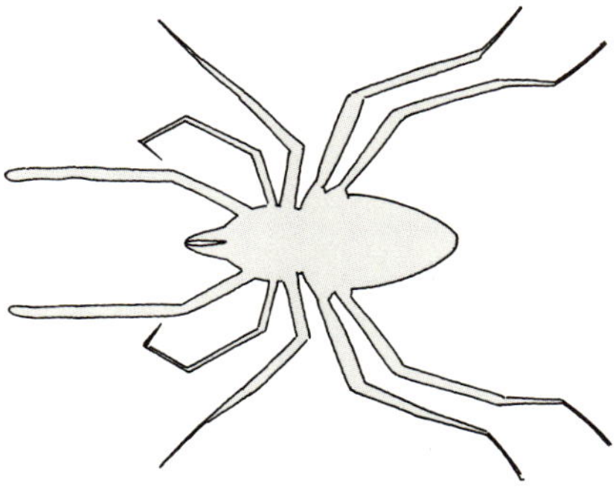

• Vividly striped in variations of yellow, black and silver; intricate 'wagon-wheel' webs; legs held together in pairs so that spider seems to have only four legs: **orb-web spider** *page 324*
• Bright yellowish or white with pink, green or brown markings; can change colour to blend with surroundings; all four legs on each side parallel to one another; always found in flowers; does not construct a web: **crab spider** *page 324*

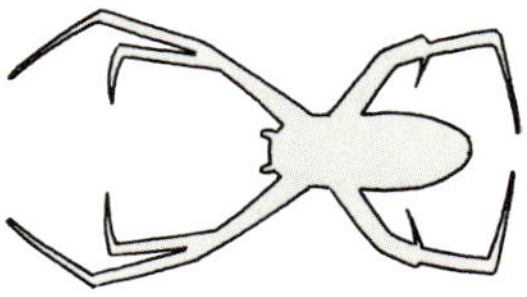

• Generally glossy brown or black, some with dark orange stripes; cylindrical body; many legs tucked neatly under body: **millipede** *page 327*
• Usually dark olive-green, black or dark bluish, sometimes red, yellow or brown; flattened body; legs spread out sideways: **centipede** *page 327*

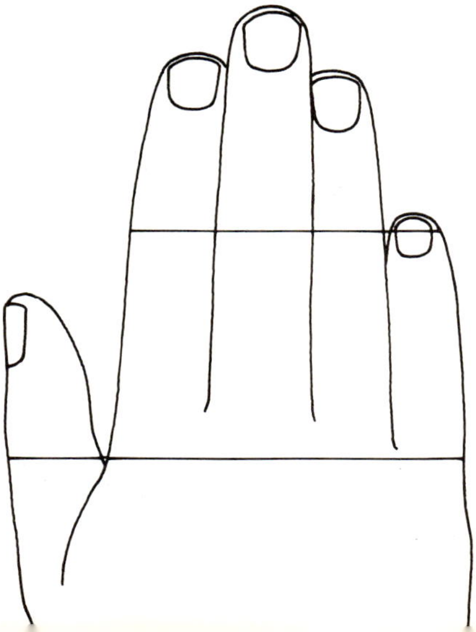

Beetles

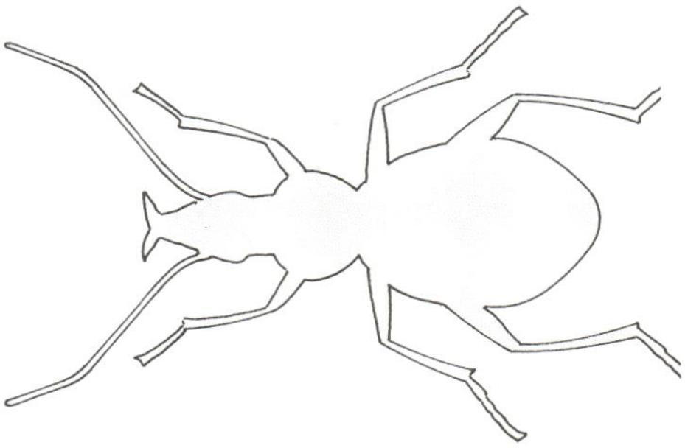

- Prominent, sabrelike mouthparts; black, often with white, yellow and red patches on the thorax or elytra (wing-cases); extremely active: **predacious ground beetle** *page 330*
- Dark brown, elongate, segmented body; wingless; tiny head; light-producing organ at tip of abdomen: **female firefly** or **glow-worm** *page 333*
- Squat, globular abdomen, which can make characteristic knocking sound; black or brown; wingless: **toktokkie** *page 334*
- Elongated snout; usually brown or black, often with a camouflage pattern of other colours; largest specimens have pink or red spots; 'elbowed' antennae: **weevil** *page 335*

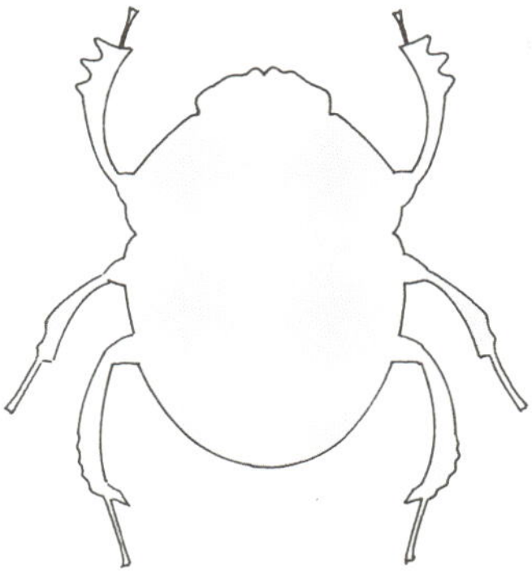

- Oval, stout; black, brown or metallic bronze, blue or green; front legs flat, toothed, used to manipulate dung: **dung beetle** *page 331*
- Flat in shape; brilliantly coloured; one common species is black, with rows of bright yellow patches on the wing-cases; another is green, with yellow bordering the wing-cases: **fruit beetle** *page 332*
- Long abdomen; usually black with bright red, orange or yellow markings; elytra brightly coloured; small thorax: **blister beetle** *page 334*

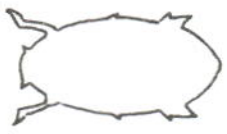

- Smooth, streamlined shape; shiny black or grey, with a paler border to the wing-cases and back in some species; four rearmost legs fringed with bristles; front pair of legs longer than the others; rarely found underwater; swims on water surface; eyes divided: **whirligig beetle** *page 330*
- Streamlined, pip-shaped bodies; pale yellow to black, or green-black with yellow margins; found underwater; eyes undivided: **water beetle** *page 331*

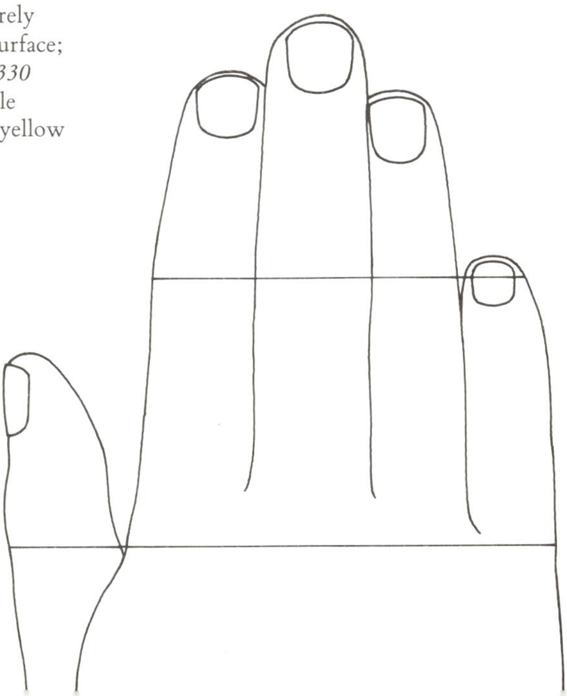

Butterflies

• Cream-yellow with greenish tinge and black spot in middle of forewing; wingspan 6-6,5 cm: **African migrant** *page 340*
• Black above with white spots and white patch on forewing; larger white patch in middle of hindwing extending onto forewing; wingspan 9-10 cm: **friar** *page 341*
• Black above with whitish or yellowish spots on forewing and large, yellowish patch on inner half of each hindwing; wingspan 5,5-7,5 cm: **chief** *page 342*
• Male black above with two white patches in forewing and one in hindwing; female orange with black wing borders and white spots in black tip to forewing; wingspan 6-7,5 cm: **diadem** *page 342*
• Orange-brown wings with black border; three or four black spots in orange hindwings; black tip to forewing with white blotches; wingspan 5-7 cm: **southern milkweed** *page 343*
• Mid-brown above, sometimes with reddish tinge; two eye-spots near outer edge of each forewing and (usually) three smaller eye-spots on hindwing; wingspan 3,9-5 cm: **marsh patroller** *page 345*
• White above with black apex to forewing and brownish black border to hindwing; bar in middle of forewing; wingspan 4-4,5 cm: **brown-veined white** *page 349*

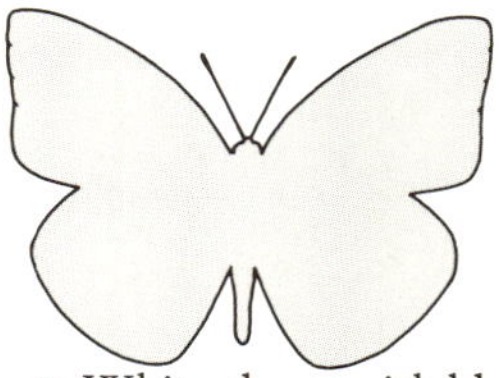

• White above with black wing margins and scarlet tip to forewing; hindwing white, with black-tipped edges; wingspan 4-5 cm: **scarlet-tip** *page 349*
• White above with black dots along outer margins of wings; undersides yellow, shading to orange near wing-bases; wingspan 5-5,5 cm: **dotted border** *page 350*
• Males orange-yellow above with broad black or dark brown margin to wings; small black spot in middle of forewing; yellow edge to inner part of hindwing. Female similar, but orange-yellow is partly obscured by brown; wingspan 3,5-4 cm: **African clouded yellow** *page 350*
• Rich yellow with a broad, blackish brown outer border to wings; wingspan 3-4 cm: **broad-bordered grass-yellow** *page 351*
• Dark brown to black above with several golden, angular spots on both fore- and hindwings; wingspan 2,5-3 cm: **gold-spotted sylph** *page 351*

• Broad black band dotted with orange along outer edges of wings; inner halves of wings orange and brick-red, dotted in places with black; two slender, sharp-pointed tails; wingspan 6-9 cm: **koppie charaxes** *page 340*
• Reddish brown outer half of wings, with two rows of yellowish spots on forewings; pearly-white inner half; short tails; wingspan 8-10 cm: **pearl charaxes** *page 344*
• Male patterned in yellow and black with broad tail to each hindwing; wingspan 7,5-9 cm: **mocker swallowtail** *page 338*

• Dark brown to black; white band across middle of hindwing; rows of black spots parallel to outer edges of wings; forewing has three white spots near tip, and two white patches in mid-wing; wingspan 4-5 cm: **small spotted sailor** *page 341*
• Red or orange-red, but outer third of each forewing clear or translucent; red inner part of forewing has two or three small black spots; hindwing has black spots; wingspan 4,5-5,5 cm: **garden acraea** *page 346*

• Pale orange, bordered narrowly in black and evenly covered with small black spots; wingspan 3-3,6 cm: **polka dot** *page 347*
• Orange with black wing margins and wing veins outlined in black; wingspan 2,4-3 cm: **mountain copper** *page 352*

Butterflies

• Whitish green with pearly lustre; wings carry purple, yellow and black eye-spots; tip of forewing bordered in black; hindwings have short tail; wingspan 6,5-9 cm: **mother-of-pearl** *page 339*
• Brown above with comma-shaped, black eye-spot (on an orange background) in apex of each forewing; wingspan 6-7 cm: **evening brown** *page 343*
• Orange with black and white markings; slightly scalloped margin to wings; wingspan 4-5 cm: **painted lady** *page 346*
• In summer red above with broad black outer margins and black at base of wings; in winter violet-blue above with black-tipped red spots parallel to outer edge of wings; outer edges of wings scalloped; wingspan 5-6 cm: **gaudy commodore** *page 347*
• Black with orange-yellow patch on each fore- and hindwing, and large, violet-blue spot in centre of each hindwing; wingspan

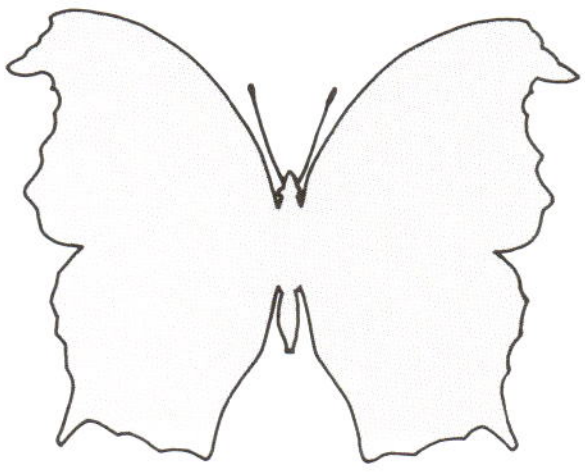

4-5 cm: **yellow pansy** *page 348*
• Black with large, blue spot in each hindwing; broken white band across each forewing; treble white band along outer edge of each hindwing; blue-centred, orange-red eye-spots on each wing; wingspan 4-5 cm: **blue pansy** *page 348*
• Outer halves of male's wings orange-red, with black border to edge of forewing, and black spots; inner halves of wings lustrous, iridescent blue-pink; wingspan 2,3-3 cm: **Thysbe copper** *page 352*

• Black with broken yellow band across each forewing and hindwing; two blue, black and orange eye-spots on each hindwing; wingspan 8-9 cm: **citrus swallowtail** *page 338*
• Dark brown with two (male) or three (female) broken orange bands parallel to outer edge of forewing and another on hindwing, which has mauve eye-spots between outer margin and orange band; wingspan 7-8 cm: **mountain pride** *page 344*
• Orange above with jagged-edged black patches extending from middle of wings to

body; black bar near outer margin of fore- and hindwing; dark wing-veins; wingspan 4-4,8 cm: **joker** *page 345*

• Inner halves of both fore- and hindwings brilliant blue, bordered on outer edges with blackish brown, shading to chestnut-brown; brown tail to each hindwing; wingspan 3-3,7 cm: **fig tree blue** *page 353*
• Bright metallic blue above with black border to wings, forming triangular patch

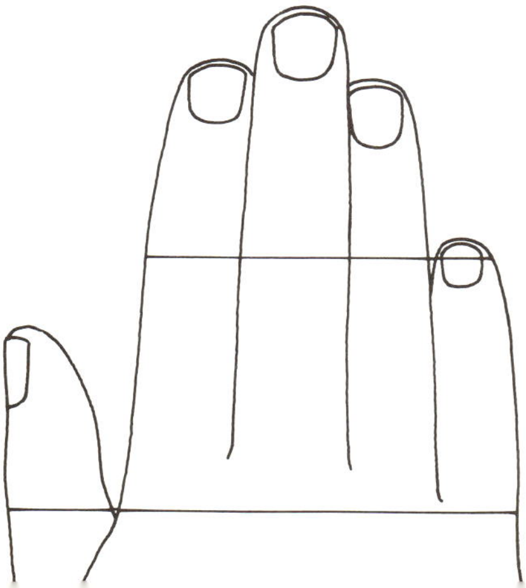

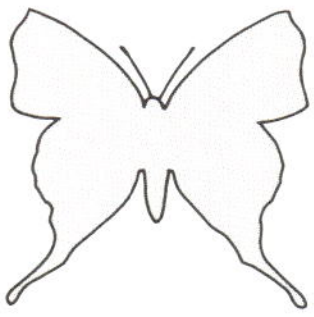

at tip of forewing; two red spots at tip of each hindwing; wingspan 3-3,6 cm: **sapphire** *page 353*
• Violet-blue with narrow brown outer border, and two small black spots at tip of hindwing; short tail; wingspan 2,5-3 cm: **lucerne blue** *page 354*
• Grey-brown with white-edged black spot at rear of each forewing and three to five more along outer margin of each hindwing; whitish tail to each hindwing; wingspan 1,8-3 cm: **tailed black-eye** *page 354*

Other insects

• Swift-flying; body brilliantly coloured; wings with dark spot near apex; short antennae: **dragonfly** *page 361*
• Slow-flying; long antennae; transparent wings often vividly patterned in brown, yellow, black and white; active mainly at night: **antlion** *page 372*

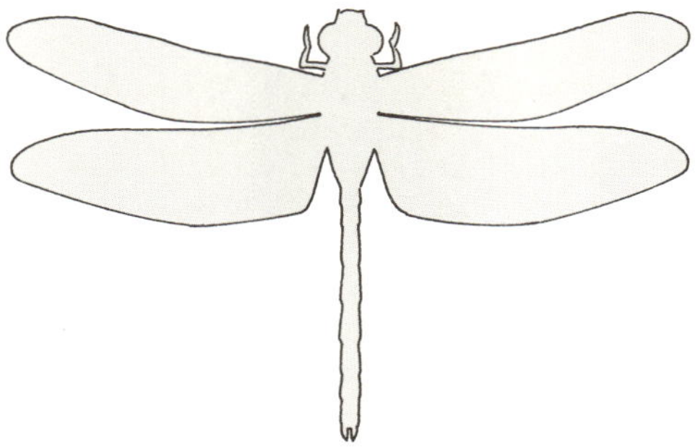

• Spiky plate over neck; dark brown, grey or reddish brown, with two narrow yellow stripes along back of abdomen: **armoured cricket** *page 364*
• Short body, dark brown or black in colour; 'chirping' song: **field cricket** *page 365*
• Forewings translucent and unpigmented; antennae longer than body; swordlike ovipositor; light green or yellow in colour: **tree cricket** *page 365*
• Compact body; digging forelegs flattened with sharp teeth; small wings; golden brown to black: **mole cricket** *page 366*
• Green, sometimes tinged with pink, and often dotted and striped with silver or red; inflated, bladderlike abdomen with dark line along belly: **bladder grasshopper** *page 366*
• Green, brown or black with bright markings; emits foul-smelling foam in response to danger; generally slow-moving: **stink locust** *page 367*
• Generally brown, varying slightly according to species and age; short, thick antennae: **locust** *page 367*

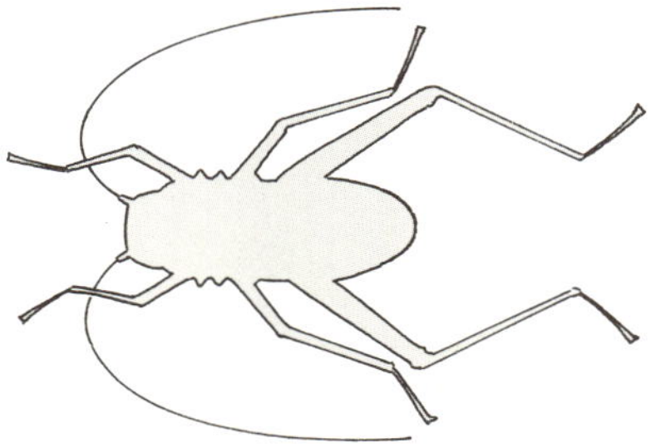

• Black or brown; slender body; female has long ovipositor; long antennae; most have wings: **ichneumon wasp** *page 377*
• Curled antennae; long hindlegs; body usually black, black-and-orange or dark brown; wings orange-brown or dark blue; jerky movements when not in flight: **spider wasp** *page 378*
• Brown body with bright markings; builds nests of paper; folds wings longitudinally when at rest; ovipositor concealed under abdomen: **social wasp** *page 378*
• Head, thorax and tip of abdomen black; long waist red; body slender; narrow wings; nests in ground: **sand wasp** *page 379*
• Reddish brown to brown; round body; male has fluffy head and thorax; large wings; often seen in columns: **driver ant** *page 380*

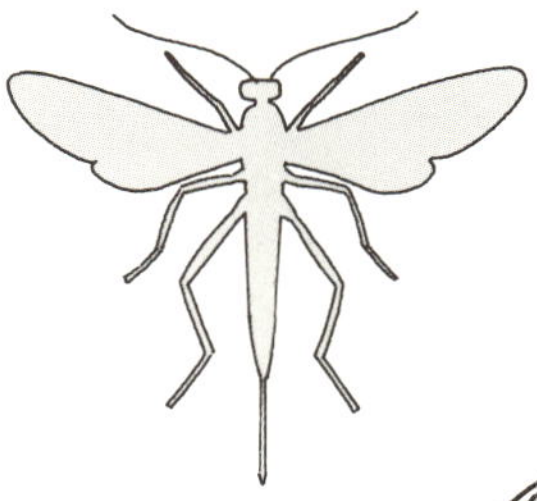

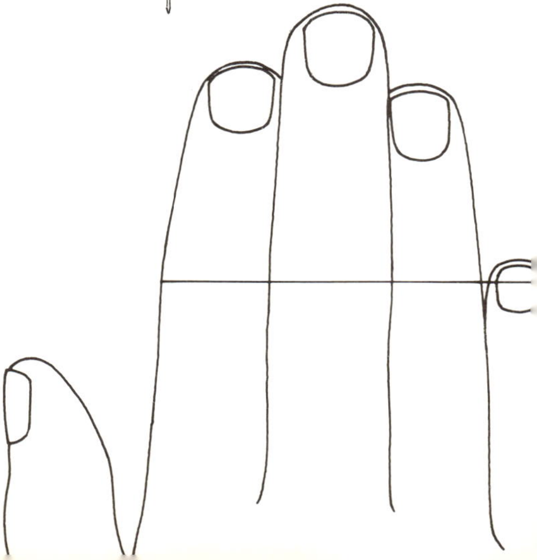

OTHER INSECTS

Other insects

• Rounded body; colour varies from brown-grey to reddish brown and pale yellow; head of soldiers large, with huge jaws acting as pincers: **termite** *page 362*
• Slim body; brown, tan, yellow or blackish; two pincers at tail end: **garden earwig** *page 363*

• Usually dark green or black, though sometimes brightly coloured; back legs adapted for jumping; nymphs produce foam or cuckoo-spit nests: **spittle bug** *page 368*
• Green, yellow or black, sometimes with orange or yellow markings; flat bodies; hard forewings; unpleasant smell if held or squashed: **shield bug** *page 369*

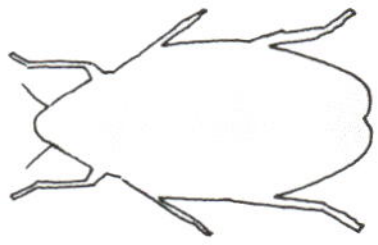

• Short, rounded abdomen; large, iridescent eyes do not meet in middle of head; generally brownish; wings held at sides of body at rest: **horsefly** *page 373*
• Large, compound eyes bulging upwards and separated at top of head by a deep trough; head turns constantly; colour generally brown; very hairy, especially about the face; one pair of wings; stout proboscis: **robber fly** *page 374*
• One pair of wings; colour brown, yellow or black with yellow stripes or spots; body usually stocky; no sting: **hoverfly** *page 374*
• Yellow, brown or black with heavily marked wings; two wings held in characteristic drooping fashion when at rest; eyes often iridescent: **fruit fly** *page 375*
• Body brown to black; small, fleshy proboscis beneath head; four dark stripes on thorax; dull wings: **housefly** *page 375*

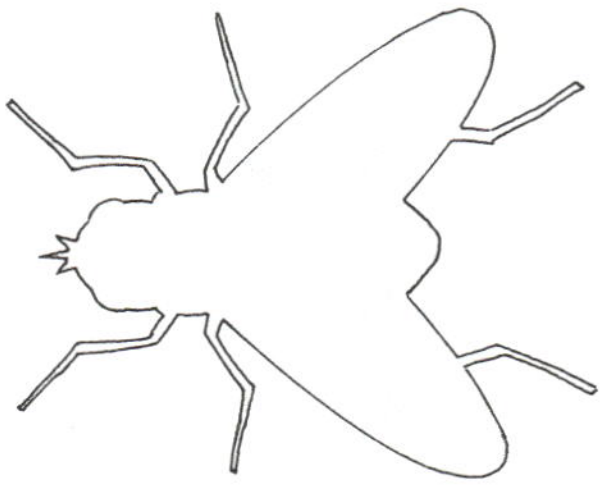

• Drab yellowish brown; mouthparts project forward and upward from under the head; wings fold across each other when at rest: **tsetse fly** *page 376*
• Body stout; brilliant blue or green; found on meat, carcasses or livestock: **blowfly** *page 376*
• Blackish brown, usually striped with yellow; often seen in swarms; sting present; two pairs of wings; pollen baskets on hindlegs: **honeybee** *page 380*

• Shiny blue-black, sometimes with bands of white, yellow or deep orange; pear-shaped abdomen (raised when alarmed); mostly arboreal: **cocktail ant** *page 381*
• Long-limbed; brown or black with whitish yellow abdomen; nests in sand: **sugar ant** *page 381*

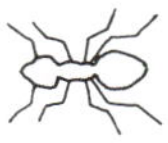

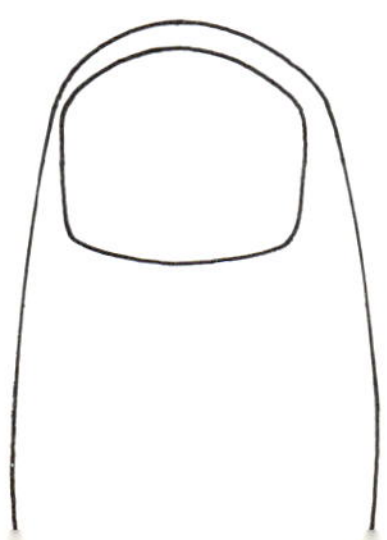